KU-314-207

The NHS
Home Healthcare
Guide

CONTENTS

Published by the National Health Service Executive in association with the Doctor-Patient Partnership and the Health Education Authority.

Developed and produced by Phase IV Communications Limited in association with the Health Education Authority.

Printed in Europe. ©Phase IV Communications Limited. 1998   ISBN 1 85839 884 3

INTRODUCTION

by Claire Rayner, Chair of the Patients' Association

Photography by Amanda Rayner

Before the birth of the NHS, most people looked after illness themselves at home. Only the most severe of problems justified getting involved with that special being 'The Doctor'. Then came the good news of the NHS, which brought medical care to everyone, free at the point of use, and much of the old family knowledge of how to cope with everyday health problems lost its importance and was discarded. This was bad news, because sensible self care remains, despite the huge strides made in medical knowledge over the past half century, the simplest, most comfortable and most effective way of being well. What's more, it's the least expensive, which has a lot going for it in these hard pressed days.

It was because of a growing awareness of the value of good self care that the Doctor-Patient Partnership, parented by the British Medical Association and the Patient's Association, was born, and why that Partnership has been involved in the production of this guide. It aims to restore that forgotten wisdom with the addition of modern knowledge, to enable families to get well when they're ill, and to stay well.

There is a wide range of information given in the *NHS Home Healthcare Guide.* Not only is there clear guidance on how to treat yourself but also on how to use all the available services there are to support your own efforts. The high street pharmacist, the community nurse, your local dentist, the optometrist, and a wide range of voluntary self help organisations covering many different conditions are all there to act as family advisors and supporters. And, of course, ultimately, there is the impressive range of modern medicine from your GP through to the most complex hospital treatments. All of this is explained in these pages, with special focus on what you can do for yourself and when you should consult your doctor, and set out in a way that makes it easy to use and follow.

Of one thing we can be sure as we reach the 50th anniversary of the birth of the NHS: patients are no longer objects *to* and *for* whom professionals provide care, but sensible, thoughtful people *with* whom the experts work to ensure enjoyable good health for all.

RESPONSIBLE SELF HELP - How to use this book

Dr Simon Fradd, Chairman of the Doctor-Patient Partnership

We all make decisions about our health - and sometimes the health of others, such as children - every day. We try our best to eat the right foods, get enough sleep, dress warmly and so on. And when illness does strike, we have to decide how to manage the problem. Do we go to bed, use a home remedy, or see the doctor?

This book will help you make the right decisions about managing illness. It is designed to give you all the information you need on treating common ailments in the home, with clear notes on when you should visit your doctor.

There are many useful home remedies that don't actually need medicines. But if you do need a medicine, there are two main groups: those available only on prescription, and those that can be bought 'over the counter'. These non-prescription medicines also fall into o groups: those available only from a pharmacy, and others which are more generally available g. in supermarkets). All medicines have to pass strict government regulations, so you can be re that the medicines you buy are safe, as long as you follow the instructions on the label refully.

step-by-step approach

llowing a step-by-step approach to self-care will help you make the right decisions, and ll save you time by cutting out unnecessary visits to the doctor. It will also help you event illness.

First, we suggest you read *A plan for healthy living* (p10-15), which gives an easy-to-follow an for keeping healthy, preventing serious diseases and reducing common minor illnesses as ach as possible.

If you do feel ill and you are pretty sure what is wrong, then go directly to the relevant page in e *Directory of common illnesses*. These are listed alphabetically in ten main sections which u will find noted on p1. The general *Index* on p62-64 will also help you find the illness you are oking for. You can also think about and identify the symptoms you have, and then refer to the *dex of signs and symptoms* (p10-11). This will help you find the right page in the *Directory of mmon illnesses*. If there is an emergency or accidental injury, go straight to *First aid* on p5-9.

You can often get extra advice from the large number of self-help groups listed under *Useful ntacts and further reading* on p59-61; many of these groups have books or leaflets with extra formation that they will send to you. There are also many books on health and illness available bookshops or libraries if you want to learn more about your condition (ask the person in charge do a computer search for you if you can't find what you want). The Internet has a lot of formation on health, but remember that not everything you read on the Internet is true.

This book does not cover all illnesses and conditions; rather it serves as a 'filter' to help you cide which illnesses can be treated at home and which need you to visit your doctor. If, after ing this book, you are still uncertain about your symptoms, then speak to your pharmacist or ctor (see p4). Keep important medical contact numbers readily available by noting them in the ace on the inside back cover.

The Doctor-Patient Partnership (DPP) was set up in 1996 to help inform the public on ow to look after their own health and, if they do become ill, how to get the most out of heir GP services. By using our health services better everyone can get excellent ealthcare when they really need it.

HELPING YOUR DOCTOR TO HELP YOU

by Dr Simon Fradd

By following eight simple tips you will be able to get the most out of the time you spend with your doctor, and make best use of all the other services your surgery provides.

1. Read your doctor's practice leaflet, which explains how the surgery works. For example it will note how much time is needed for repeat prescriptions, and who will do simple tests like measuring blood pressure - it may be a nurse.
2. Be prepared. Read this book and refer to it when you're ill.
3. Find out when your surgery is open, so that you know when you can make an appointment or get a prescription.
4. Keep your appointment or cancel it. If you can't keep an appointment with your doctor nurse, let your surgery know as soon as possible.
5. Think about why you are going to see the doctor, and make a note of what you want to discuss.
6. If you are nervous or worried, you may not remember what the doctor tells you, so take friend or relative with you.
7. Ask questions if you don't understand anything. If necessary, ask your doctor to write down the answers and explanations.
8. Think twice if you have a minor ailment. Do you really need to see your doctor? Have you tried the simple home remedies listed in this guide? Few illnesses need urgent medical attention, so try not to call out your doctor on an unnecessary visit to your home

Help your doctor and surgery to have more time to help you when you really need it by followir these guidelines. Also, check with your surgery whether you can phone in for advice.

> If you have a complaint about your medical treatment, your surgery will be able to tell you what to do. You can also call your local *Community Health Council* (called the *Local Health Council* in Scotland and the *Central Services Agency* in N Ireland) for advice (number in local phone book).

HOW YOUR PHARMACIST CAN HELP

by Dr Alison Blenkinsopp

Your pharmacist is there to advise you about medicines, including remedies for common ailments. They are also able to tell you when you need to see a doctor.

So, go and see your pharmacist first if:

1. You need help choosing the right medicine
2. You are not sure what is causing a problem or what to do about it
3. You are unsure whether you need to see a doctor
4. You want advice on how to stay healthy.

To help your pharmacist help you, stick to the same pharmacy. That way you will get to know the pharmacist and staff, and they will get to know you. Note your pharmacy's telephone number in the space left at the back of this book - you can always get advice over the phone - and read your pharmacy leaflet which will tell you about opening times, urgent prescriptions etc.

When you are thinking of buying a medicine, remember some medicines don't mix. Be sure to te your pharmacist if you are taking other medicines. All staff in pharmacies have had special training about medicines. If you ask for a medicine, you will be asked a few questions to check out that the one you have chosen is right for you. Be sure to give the information they need.

With the specialist advice of your pharmacist and the very effective medicines you can buy in pharmacies these days, you can treat yourself and save yourself time and inconvenience. So, make the most of your pharmacist.

FIRST AID *by the British Red Cross*

Most accidental injuries are minor and can be treated using simple first aid measures. But in the unlikely event of a serious accident or sudden illness, knowledge of first aid techniques could help you to save someone's life.

Accidents can be prevented. Simple measures like smoke detectors, non-slip bath mats, and safe storage of medicines and toxic materials can help. It's also wise to keep basic first aid materials easily available in your *Home Medicine Chest* (see p57-58).

Basic first aid items
- A selection of 20 plasters in assorted sizes.
- six medium, two large and two extra-large sterile dressings.
- triangular bandages.
- two sterile eye pads.
- cotton wool, safety pins, tweezers, sharp scissors and disposable gloves.

By following the basic guidelines provided here you will be able to deal with most day-to-day accidents and injuries. Information on dealing with emergencies is also provided. To get more detailed information, and training in emergency first aid, contact the *The British Red Cross* or *St John's Ambulance* (see p60).

Emergencies

Seek URGENT medical attention for:
- Head injury with bleeding from eyes, ears or nose, drowsiness or vomiting
- Loss of consciousness
- Broken bone or dislocation
- Severe chest pain or breathlessness
- Sudden severe stomach pain that won't go away
- Unresolved choking and difficulty breathing
- Severe bleeding.

The main things to remember in any emergency situation are:
- remain calm and confident
- do all you can to help but don't put yourself in danger
- do not give the patient anything to eat or drink.

Getting help
Sometimes, the quickest way of getting medical help is to take the patient directly to the accident department of your local hospital. But call an ambulance and do not move the patient if:
- You think he or she may have a back or neck injury, or any other injury that could be made worse by movement
- The person is in shock, unconscious or has stopped breathing, and needs your constant attention
- The person has severe chest pain or breathlessness (see p6).

The recovery position
This is a safe position for an unconscious person, which allows easy breathing and prevents choking if the patient vomits. After checking the person is breathing normally, turn them on their side. Ensure the airway is open with the jaw pulled forward and their head tipped slightly back. Note that one hand supports the head.

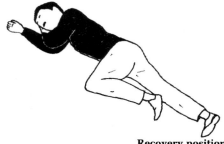

Recovery position

Mouth-to-mouth resuscitation

A person may stop breathing for many different reasons, including drowning, electric shock or poisoning. A few simple steps can save their life:

1. Lay the person on a firm surface. Tilt back the head and lift the chin to open the air passages. Remove any false teeth and send for help if possible.
2. Check to see if they are breathing for 10 seconds. If they are, place them in the recovery position described on p5
3. If they are still not breathing, pinch the nose shut. Take a deep breath and place your mouth firmly over the patient's mouth. Breathe into the mouth twice - the chest should rise.
4. Continue to give a breath every 6 seconds (about 10 times a minute). In a young child, breathe gently once every 3 seconds. In a baby, cover both nose and mouth with your mouth.
5. Do not stop until the person breathes alone or medical help arrives.

There is no evidence of HIV or hepatitis being passed on during mouth-to-mouth resuscitation, but use a mask or face shield if the casualty's mouth or nose is bleeding, as HIV is spread by blood-to-blood contact.

Cardio-pulmonary resuscitation (CPR)

CPR is a life-saving technique for a person whose heart (pulse) has stopped. It's best used only if you have been trained in the technique (Contact the *British Red Cross* or *St John's Ambulance*, p60, for more information).

Chest pain

Pain in the chest is most often caused by indigestion (see p30). However, severe chest pain, together with other symptoms, may be a sign of insufficient oxygen reaching the heart (angina), or a heart attack, which is caused by sudden blockage of the blood supply to the heart. The symptoms of both are a vice-like pain in the middle of the chest, often spreading down the left arm and the jaw. The pain may be accompanied by shortness of breath, sudden faintness or giddiness, 'ash grey' skin and blueness of the lips, and a feeling of anxiety.

Severe chest pain needs urgent attention. Sit the person down, make them comfortable and help them use any medicine they normally take for angina (usually tablets or a 'puffer' aerosol). **If the pain does not ease within minutes, or if it returns, do not try to contact your own doctor. Ring 999 and wait for help to arrive.** If the person affected is fully conscious and not known to have a problem with aspirin, give them one tablet to chew slowly. Be prepared to resuscitate if the person collapses.

Shock

People who have experienced an injury may go into shock. They may become pale, sweaty, drowsy and confused. **A person in shock needs urgent medical attention.** While waiting for help, remain calm and reassure the patient, but do not give them anything to eat or drink. If they are conscious, lay the person on their back with their legs raised, loosen any tight clothing and keep them warm. An unconscious person who is breathing should be placed in the recovery position (p5).

Bites and stings

Insect bites and stings can be painful but they are not usually serious, even in children. Most can be treated with simple remedies without needing the attention of your doctor.

Apply a cold compress to insect bites and stings. Suck on an ice cube or sip cold water if you're stung in the mouth and **seek immediate medical attention.** Remove bee stings with tweezers by gripping the base of the sting nearest to the skin to avoid squeezing the poison sac. Wasps do not leave a sting. Remove ticks by covering them with a smear of vaseline, which blocks their breathing holes, and causes them to drop off. Simply pulling at the tick

Broken bones and dislocations

Broken bones and dislocations always need immediate medical attention. They can be very painful, and you can help by keeping the patient calm and still.

Broken limbs
Steady and support the limb with your hands. If a leg is broken, place padding around it to prevent movement. A broken arm or collar bone should be supported on the affected side of the body.

Injured neck or spine
Keep the injured person as still as possible. It is essential not to move someone with a neck or spine injury unless they are in imminent danger of further injury. If the casualty becomes unconscious, carefully place them in recovery position (p5) while keeping the spine in line at all times (i.e. do not twist their neck or back).

Dislocated joints
Never try to force a joint back into place. Simply support the limb and seek emergency help.

Burns and scalds

Any burn or scald requires immediate action. For minor injuries, carefully remove watches, jewellery, shoes and anything else that may cause constriction if swelling occurs. Cool the affected area with cold water for at least 10 minutes, then cover with a light, non-fluffy material. For a limb, kitchen film or a polythene bag may be used. Don't burst any blisters and don't apply any cream or ointments. The exception is mild sunburn which may be soothed with a lotion like calamine.

Seek medical attention if:
- the burn is larger than the size of your hand
- the burn is on the face
- the skin is broken.

or trying to burn it off can leave the head in the skin, leading to infection.

Seek medical attention if:
- you have a known allergy to bites and stings
- the sting cannot be removed
- there is infection around the affected area
- you experience shortness of breath or fever.

Animal bites
Animal bites need urgent medical attention, as they may become infected if not treated. Small animal bites should be thoroughly cleaned with soap and water and covered with a sterile dressing. For serious bites, apply direct pressure with a clean cloth (as described on p8) to control the bleeding. If you are bitten by an animal abroad, seek immediate medical attention. Also, have the police catch the animal to make sure it does not have rabies.

Anaphylactic shock is an extreme allergic reaction that causes itching and swelling of the lips and throat, anxiety, a red blotchy skin, difficulty breathing and a rapid pulse. **It's a medical emergency and you should phone 999 immediately.**

Severe burns need urgent medical attention. Cool the burn down, cover it with a sterile dressing, and **get the patient to your local accident and emergency department immediately or call for an ambulance.** While waiting for the ambulance, lay the person down and raise their legs. This helps keep blood available for the vital organs. Don't remove clothes if they are sticking to the skin.

Choking

Choking happens surprisingly often. Immediate action is vital, so it is important to know the correct steps to follow:

1. Check inside the mouth, and remove any obstruction
2. If you can't see or feel any obstruction, bend the patient over and use the flat of your hand to slap them firmly between the shoulder blades five times to dislodge the blockage; use a more gentle tap for small children
3. If choking continues, try the abdominal thrust: stand behind the patient, put both arms around their waist and interlock your hands. Then pull sharply upwards below the ribs, telling them to cough as you do so. Do not use this technique on a baby under 12 months old
4. Repeat this procedure until the blockage is removed
5. If the blockage is not completely cleared, or the patient continues to have trouble breathing, seek urgent medical attention.

Cuts, grazes and bleeding

For a minor cut, press the wound with a clean fabric pad for a few minutes to help stop the bleeding. For a cut on an arm or leg, elevate the limb. Use water to wipe around the edge of the cut or graze. Once clean, apply a dressing, e.g. a plaster.

Seek medical attention if:
■ The cut is deep and the edges cannot be pulled together
■ Severe redness or swelling develops

after a couple of days (this may be a sign of an infection).

Severe bleeding from a wound needs immediate medical attention. While waiting for expert help, lay the person down and raise the injured part of the body above the level of the heart to help reduce blood loss. Place a clean cloth against the wound and press firmly. Secure this pad in place. **Never use a tourniquet.**

Nose bleeds

Nose bleeds are common and most are easily dealt with. Sit the person down, leaning slightly forward, and tell them to breathe through the mouth. Then pinch the soft part of the nose firmly for about 10 minutes. Seek medical help if the bleeding continues for more than 30 minutes or if you suspect the nose is broken.

Fits and convulsions

Fits are usually caused by fever or epilepsy. Convulsions due to fever are common in babies and young children, usually owing to high temperatures (see p46). While fits can look alarming, a single fit caused by high temperature is usually not serious. If a person has a fit, remove any hard or sharp objects near them, loosen tight clothing and protect their head. **Never restrain the person or insert anything between their teeth.** After a fit, place the person in the recovery position (p5). If they are feverish, sponge them with lukewarm water.

Seek medical attention if:
■ It is a first fit for a baby or child
■ The convulsions lasted longer than 5 minutes.

Head injuries

Bangs on the head are common, particularly amongst children. Few need the attention of your doctor, but occasionally a head injury can cause bleeding inside the skull, which needs urgent attention. This bleeding can take place soon after the injury, or up to 6 months later.

For a minor knock or bump to the head, t the person down as they may be dizzy, nd place a cold, damp cloth on the affected rea. You may want to provide a basin in ase the patient vomits.

Seek urgent medical attention if:
- The person experiences double vision or hearing loss
- Repeated vomiting, fits or convulsions occur
- The patient seems confused
- Blood or colourless discharge appears from the nose, eyes or ears
- The pain continues after 3 days.

Remember that these symptoms can appear as long as 6 months after the initial ncident. If they do, visit your doctor.

Poisoning

ccidental poisoning is one of the most ommon reasons for children to need mergency treatment, but adults also equire urgent medical assistance. **Seek xpert medical advice immediately.** You an provide important help for the doctors y trying to find out what has caused the oisoning, how much was taken and when, nd by taking any containers and remains of blets, liquids, plants or samples of vomit o the hospital with you. Do not make the atient vomit

If the patient becomes unconscious, lace them in the recovery position (p5) nd if breathing stops, begin mouth-to- outh resuscitation following the rocedure described on p6.

Sprains, strains and bruises

prains and strains often occur during veryday tasks in the house or garden, or hile playing sport. To remember how to eal with a sprain, strain or bruising, think of 'RICE' (rest, ice, compress, elevation).
- **Rest** the injured part as much as possible.
- Immediately after the injury, pack the area with **ice** wrapped in a cloth - a bag of frozen peas works well - to reduce swelling. Keep the ice in place for about 20 minutes.
- Gently **compress** the injury and bind the area with a bandage (preferably elastic) so it is well supported, but make sure you don't restrict blood flow.
- To minimise swelling, keep the injured part **elevated** as much of the time as possible.

Be patient with sprains and strains: they don't heal overnight. When the pain subsides, exercise the limb or joint gently to prevent stiffness. Only resume normal activities when there is no pain or swelling. Bruising also takes several days to get better. It will start off blue, purple or black, fading to yellow before it disappears.

Seek medical attention if:
- You think there may be a broken bone; immobilise the area with padding and seek aid immediately
- Symptoms don't improve
- Bruising remains after several days.

➡ **Fits - p46**   ➡**Useful contacts - p60**
➡ **Home Medicine Chest - p57**

First aid

A PLAN FOR HEALTHY LIVING

It's easy to take your health for granted until something starts to go wrong, but prevention is far better than cure. By taking steps to follow a healthy lifestyle now, you can reduce your risk of getting serious illnesses. A healthy lifestyle also improves day to day living. You will feel better, your skin and hair will be in better condition, and it will help boost your immune system so that you get fewer minor illnesses.

Although the information in this book is relevant to disabled people and their carers, they may need extra specialist advice to help maximise their quality of life and general health. A number of organisations are listed on p59-61, which will be able to provide this additional information, advice and support.

Choose life, not smoking

The facts about smoking:

- More than 120,000 people die each year (about 300 a day) from illnesses due to smoking. Those who smoke more than 25 cigarettes a day are 25 times more likely to die from lung cancer and almost twice as likely to die from heart disease
- Smoking reduces fertility, causes the menopause to start about 2 years earlier in women, and increases the risk of getting osteoporosis
- Passive smoking is harmful and is the cause of serious respiratory illnesses, middle ear disease and asthmatic attacks in babies and children. Sudden infant death is twice as common in smoking households.

It's never too late to stop smoking. Smokers who stop increase their chance of living a longer, healthier life, and reduce their risk of having a heart attack or getting cancer.

A plan to stop smoking

- Name the day you'll give up. If possible, get a relative or friend to give up at the same time.
- Throw away your cigarettes, matches, lighters, ashtrays etc.
- Take it one day at a time - keep a chart and tick off each day without a cigarette.
- Do something to keep your hands busy (e.g. model making, painting or DIY).
- Avoid situations where you used to smoke.
- Learn to say "No thanks, I don't smoke" and mean it, and ask people around you to help.
- Save the money you would have spent on cigarettes, and spend it on a treat for yourself after 1 month of not smoking.
- Ask your pharmacist or doctor about nicotine replacement products if you find the going tough, or contact *Quit* (p59) for more tips on how to give up and how to join your local 'stop smoking' group.
- If you have problems giving up, consult your practice nurse or GP for help.

The Green Paper *Our Healthier Nation* sets out a *Contract for Health* which shows how central government, local organisations and individuals all have important roles to play in improving health for everyone in England. Copies of *Our Healthier Nation* are available from the Stationery Office, or on the Department of Health's Internet site (see p59)

Drug abuse

The abuse of drugs, gases, glue and aerosols is dangerous. It usually occurs in teenagers, so try to teach your child about the danger of drugs long before they are tempted to try any (contact the *National Drugs Helpline*, p59, for more information). See your doctor if you think your child may be abusing drugs.

Signs to look out for are sudden changes in mood, unusual irritability or aggression, loss of appetite, loss of interest in hobbies, sport, school or friends, and bouts of drowsiness or sleepiness. Many of these signs can be confused with those of normal growing up. So, don't jump to the wrong conclusions, and try to be sure of your facts before doing anything.

Eat well and stay trim

Being overweight affects your whole life and increases your chance of developing serious illnesses. Check the height/weight chart below to give you some idea of what a healthy weight is for your height. If you are overweight, a combination of healthy eating, physical activity and moderate drinking, will get your body into shape. But, don't take dieting too far, being underweight can be just as bad as being overweight. Refusing to eat (anorexia) and forced vomiting after eating (bulimia) are serious illnesses and need medical help; there are also organisations that will be able to help (e.g. *Eating Disorders Association*, p59).

Height/weight chart

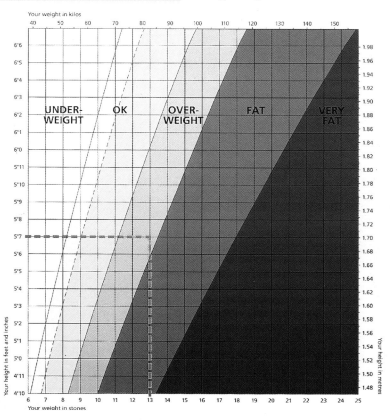

Alcohol and your health

For men over 40 years, and women who have been through the menopause, a moderate alcohol intake - 1 to 2 units per day - may protect against risk of heart disease. But, if you regularly drink more than you should, your chance of having health problems (e.g. heart disease, liver damage, and mouth and throat cancers) increases. Men should drink no more than 3-4 units of alcohol a day, while women should drink no more than 2-3 units a day. If you have a problem with alcohol, *Alcoholics Anonymous* or *Drinkline*, p59, will be able to give you support and advice.

1 unit of alcohol is equal to:
- 100 ml (one small glass) of wine *or*
- 50 ml (one measure) of sherry *or*
- 25 ml (one tot) of spirit *or*
- 300 ml (half a pint) of normal strength beer.

Remember, we often pour more generous measures at home.

Wise eating

A healthy diet is essential for staying well, and for keeping many illnesses at bay. The Balance of Good Health plate (below) shows the types of foods and the different amounts you need to eat for a well-balanced diet.

Fruit and vegetables

Bread, other cereals and potatoes

The Balance of Good Health

Meat, fish and alternatives

Foods containing fat
Foods containing sugar

Milk and dairy foods

Tips for healthy eating

- Don't eat too much fat, especially food high in saturated fat. Choose low fat foods like low fat spreads and semi-skimmed milk. Grill rather than fry your food.
- Eat fish at least twice a week. Choose oily fish (e.g. salmon, trout, sardines, mackerel, pilchards) once a week.
- Starchy foods like bread, other cereals and potatoes should form the main part of your meals. Choose wholemeal or brown versions when possible.
- Eat at least five servings of fruit and vegetables a day, and eat a wide variety of them. They can be fresh, frozen, canned, dried or as juice (only one serving as juice counts towards the five).
- Don't eat sugary, fatty foods like chocolate, sweets, cakes and biscuits too often.
- Eat less salt. Cut down on salty foods like crisps, bacon, and tinned and packet sauces. Use less salt in cooking, and flavour your foods with herbs, spices and black pepper.
- Eat a wide variety of foods to ensure that you enjoy a healthy diet. For more information, get a copy of the booklet *Enjoy healthy eating,* from the *HEA* (p59).

1 serving of fruit or vegetables is equal to:
- 1 piece of medium-sized fruit
- 1 dessert bowlful of salad
- 1 glass (150ml) of fruit juice
- 2 tablespoonfuls of vegetables.

Physical activity

Physical activity can help to improve the quality and length of your life. People who build activity into their daily lives are less likely to suffer from stress or serious diseases.

Aim to build up to half an hour of moderate activity a day (the activity should make you feel warm and breathe more heavily than usual). Choose an activity you enjoy – for example, DIY, walking, gardening or swimming. Start off slowly and build up, check with your doctor first if you have any health problems or concerns. For more information, contact your local health promotion unit (look under Health Authority in the phone book) for a copy of the booklet Getting active, feeling fit.

Protect against the sun

Skin cancer is a major problem in the UK. The main culprit is too much sun exposure, especially during childhood. The following measures will help protect you from the sun. Don't burn - cover up with loose, light clothing, and stay in the shade - take special care to do this for babies and children. Avoid the hottest hours - 11am to 3pm. Use a high factor sunscreen (SPF15 or above) before you go out and use plenty of it. Also, use a waterproof sunscreen when swimming. Sunbeds should not be used for tanning.

Keeping mentally fit

Few people are blessed with a happy mood all the time. Mood swings are a normal part of everyday life, but sometimes they can get out of hand. One in eight men and one in five women will suffer from severe depression at some time during their life. If you develop any emotional symptoms that worry you (e.g. low mood, crying for no obvious reason, difficulty sleeping, early morning waking, no appetite for food, sex or life) see your doctor for help and advice. There are also a number of specialist organisations which can give you support and information (see p61).

Good sleeping habits

Insomnia is a common sleep disorder, affecting over five million people in the UK. It is when you find it difficult to fall asleep, or can't stay asleep. The following measures will help you get a good night's sleep:
- Don't nap during the day
- Regular physical activity can help you sleep
- Cut out substances like caffeine, cigarettes and alcohol that keep you awake
- Take time to unwind from the stresses of the day before going to bed
- Go to bed at the same time each night and get up at the same time each morning
- Make sure your bed is comfortable, and your bedroom warm, dark and quiet
- If you can't sleep, get up and read or watch the TV for a while. When you feel sleepy, go back to bed and try again.

Sexual health

About one in three pregnancies in the UK are unplanned. Many different types of contraception are available and your doctor, practice nurse or family planning clinic (number in the local phone book) will help you choose the best method for you. Emergency contraception - from your GP or local family planning clinic, or most sexual health (GUM) clinics or some A & E departments out of hours - can help to prevent pregnancy if you have had unprotected sex. The emergency contraceptive pill must be taken up to 72 hours (3 days) after unprotected sex, or the IUD must be fitted within 5 days. Contact the CES helpline for more information (see p61).

Anyone can get a sexually transmitted infection if they have unprotected sex with someone who is infected. These infections are common and there are often no obvious symptoms. Get medical advice straight away if you think you or your partner might have an infection. Most can be quickly and easily treated but some can cause serious problems like infertility if not treated. You can get free, confidential treatment and advice from any NHS *Sexual Health (GUM) Clinic* (see p61). Male and female condoms, used on their own or with other contraceptive methods, can help protect against sexually transmitted infections, including HIV, if used properly every time you have sex.

Sexual problems are common, about one in five people experience them at some time. You may lose interest in sex. Men may find they can't get an erection or come too quickly, and women may have difficulty reaching orgasm. Possible causes include stress, tiredness, anxiety, too much alcohol and recreational drugs. Talk about the problem with your partner and try changing your lifestyle. If the problem continues, see your doctor.

Vaccinations

Immunisation prepares our bodies to fight against potentially serious diseases in case we come into contact with them in the future. It's very important that your child receives each vaccination at the right time to give them the best protection.

Vaccination schedule for children

Age	Vaccine	What it does
2 months	First DTP and Hib injection First Polio (drops by mouth)	DTP protects against Diphtheria, Tetanus, Pertussis (whooping cough). Hib protects against *Haemophilus influenzae* B (which can cause respiratory infection and meningitis)
3 months	Second DTP/Hib Second Polio	
4 months	Third DTP/Hib Third Polio	
12-15 months	First MMR injection	Protects against Measles, Mumps and Rubella (german measles)
3-5 years, pre-school boosters	DT booster injection Polio booster (drops) Second MMR injection	DT protects against Diphtheria and Tetanus
10-14 years	BCG	Protects against Tuberculosis, may be given to infants, if necessary
13-18 years	Tetanus, Diphtheria and Polio boosters	

People - especially older people - with long-term health problems should ask their doctors about having flu vaccinations each year (see p22), and a vaccination against pneumonia. It's also important for women who are planning a pregnancy to have a blood test to check if they are immune to german measles (see Pregnancy screening, below).

Attending for health screening

To enjoy life fully, it's important to give yourself a regular service just as you would with a car. See your optometrist every year for an eye test, and visit your dentist at least once a year for a check up (see p19). Make an appointment with your practice nurse so you can have your blood pressure and urine checked for any sign of illness. Your nurse will tell you how often these checks need to be repeated. A routine check is available to you when you first register with a GP.

It's advisable for women to take up offers of health screening they receive from their surgery, such as cervical smears and breast checks (see p54). And don't forget the self-checks that you can do yourself at home. Men should check their testicles once a month (see p56), and women should remain breast aware (see p54).

Planning a pregnancy

Any woman who is planning a baby or who thinks she is pregnant should increase the amount of the B vitamin folic acid she eats (to protect her baby against spina bifida and other neural tube defects) by doing all of the following:

- choose foods with extra folic acid added (e.g. many breakfast cereals and some breads)
- eat foods with lots of folic acid (e.g. green leafy vegetables)
- take a vitamin supplement of 400 micrograms (mcg) folic acid each day from before you get pregnant until the twelfth week of pregnancy.

When you're planning to have a baby, it's important not to take potentially harmful substances like alcohol, cigarettes or recreational drugs. Try to avoid taking unnecessary medicines - non-prescription medicines will have warnings if they should not be used in pregnancy.

It's very important that before trying to become pregnant, women ensure they are in the best of health by following the above advice. It's also wise to talk through any concerns you have with your GP, and to check whether specific tests or specialist advice may be of value. For example, it's important for all women to check they are immune to rubella (german measles).

Stay healthy into old age

Ageing is a natural process that begins the moment we're born. Everyone ages differently but by following 'the plan for healthy living' throughout your years you can stay active and well into old age. And it's even more important once you reach your later years. Eat healthily and try to build some activity into your daily life, like brisk walking. Remember, any activity which makes you feel warm and breathe slightly more heavily than usual will help you feel and look good. The body is more likely to get ill in old age, so keep warm and follow your doctor's advice. Older people may need different amounts of medicines, so always check the label for how much to take. For more advice on getting the most out of old age, contact one of the support groups available (p59).

➡ **Men's health - p55**   ➡ **Useful contacts - p59**
➡ **Women's health - p50**

INDEX OF SIGNS AND SYMPTOMS

This index refers to the signs and symptoms listed in the *Directory of common illnesses* (pp18-56) and can be used to help you identify common ailments by recognising the signs. Simply look for the sign or symptom (in blue) which best describes what you are feeling, then look down the list of more detailed descriptions and refer to the relevant page. This is not a comprehensive guide and you should consult your doctor if there is any doubt.

Bleeding
blood in phlegm with cough, 24
blood in sperm, 56
from anus, 31
in mouth, 19
when scratching feet, 34
with diarrhoea, 29

Breathlessness
after exercise, 33
with chest pain, 6
with cough, 24
with eye irritation, 26
with wheezing, 25, 27

Change in appearance
black stools, 33
colour or shape in moles, 38
growths on hands or feet, 40
hair loss, 38, 55
pale skin, blueness of lips, with chest pain, 6
paleness of skin, lips etc, 33
pitted or loose nails, 38
small growths on genitals, 40
thickening of nails, 38
toenails discoloured, 34
weight gain (women), 52

Change in appearance (infants & children)
face turning blue, 46
turning red, 49

Change in behaviour, mood change, 11
craving for certain foods, 52
depression (in women), 52
in children with fever, 22
irritability (in women), 52
less frequent bowel movements, 28

Change in behaviour (infants & children)

confusion, 46
difficult to wake, 47
dislike of bright lights, 47
distressed crying, 49
excessive thirst, 44
incontinence, 46
refusing feeds, 47
shaking, 46, 49
unusual cry, 47

Change (general)
excessive sweating, 27
fast heartbeat, 33
heavy periods, 51
irregular periods, 51
loose stools, 28
no period, 51, 54
poor flow of urine (men), 56
problems with erection, 55
smelly feet, 34
urine bloodstained or foul smelling, 50

Change (general) (infants & children)
loose stools, 44

Coughing
chesty, 22
dry, 23, 24
painful, 24
with back pain, 18
with green phlegm, 24
with mucus, 27

Diarrhoea
with pain in abdomen, 31

Discharge
from ear, 41
from eye, 42
from penis, 56
from vagina, 51, 53

Discomfort
bloated feeling (women), 52
blocked feeling in ear, 41
breast tenderness (women),

52
chest, 26
constant feeling of full bladder, 50
dull ache in lower back region, 51
excessive wind, 30
feeling full/bloated, 30
gritty feeling in eye, 42
indigestion, with skin problems, 26
motions difficult to pass, 28
vaginal, 53
when swallowing, 25

Dizziness
with pale colour, 33

Fatigue/Tiredness
with skin problems, 26
difficulty with sleeping, 13

Feeling sick
with headache, 19
with pain in abdomen (women), 51

Fever/High temperature
with headache, 22
with joint/muscle pain, 22
with loose stools, 28

Fever/High temperature (infants & children)
generally, 46, 47, 48
constant, 44
slight, with rash, 43

Irritation/Itchiness
around anus at night, 32
caused by cosmetics or jewellery, 36
eyelid, 42
eyes, 26
inside of elbows or knees, 35
skin, 26

BACK AND NECK PAIN

Thousands of people have back and neck pain, but usually there's no problem with the spine and medical treatment is not needed. Occasionally, back and neck pain can be due to a serious problem, so visit your doctor if you have any of the signs listed under 'Consult your doctor if'.

Signs and symptoms

Non-serious back and neck pain can cause any of the following symptoms:
- Pain in one spot of the upper or lower back, often worse when you bend or cough
- Pain spreading down the back of the thigh to the ankle (sciatica)
- A stiff or painful neck.

If you are upset or have pain somewhere else, the back or neck pain may feel worse.

Causes

Most back and neck pain is caused by stiffness or spasm in the muscles around the spine. This is usually caused by doing activities you are not used to, or by sleeping in an uncomfortable position. Other causes include:
- Pregnancy
- Being overweight
- Incorrect techniques (e.g. lifting)
- One of the discs between the bones of your spine moving out of position and pressing on a nerve (sciatica).

Prevention

- Keep active. A strong back is less likely to get damaged by normal day to day activities.
- Change your position every so often if you have to stand, sit or stoop for a long time.
- Sleep on a firm mattress.
- Lift correctly - crouch down, and then straighten your knees, while keeping your back straight. If your job involves heavy lifting, ask for proper training.
- Keep to a healthy weight (see p11).

Home treatment

- Stay in bed for a day or two at the most. Too much bed rest will cause your muscles to stiffen and lose strength.
- Apply warmth, and massage the painful area.
- Take a painkiller like paracetamol or an anti-inflammatory like ibuprofen.
- Take gentle exercise (e.g. swimming on your back).
- Make sure your posture is good. If necessary, get advice from a physiotherapist.
- Don't be stressed. Try gentle relaxation or exercises such as yoga.
- Lose weight if you're overweight (see p11).
- Do exercises to strengthen your stomach, neck, back and side muscles. Write to the *National Back Pain Association*, p60, for more information.

Consult your doctor if:

- The pain goes on for more than a week
- The pain extends into one or both legs or arms
- The pain came on with no cause
- Your bottom, arms or legs are numb or tingling
- It's difficult to move any arm or leg
- Coughing or sneezing makes the pain worse
- You do not have normal bladder or bowel control.

➡ **Physical activity - p13**   ➡**Wise eating - p12**
➡**Useful contacts - p60**

DENTAL PAIN AND TOOTH CARE

Teeth can last a lifetime and problems can be avoided by following simple preventive measures.

Signs and symptoms

- Bleeding and tender gums.
- A constant ache or pain affecting one or a few teeth.
- Sensitivity to hot, cold or acid food.
- Soreness when you press the tooth.

Complications

Tooth decay is caused by sugars in the diet. Bacteria on the teeth (plaque) turn the sugar into acid which causes decay, pain and eventual infection. Gum disease is caused mainly by poor tooth brushing leading to plaque build-up.This causes inflammation and bleeding, and eventually the tooth may become loose and painful.

Prevention

Help avoid problems by:

- Brushing teeth at least twice a day with fluoride toothpaste. Use a small, soft-to-medium textured brush and change it at least every 3 months.
- Avoiding sugar-sweetened food and drinks between meals.
- Having a dental check-up at least once a year.

Children should have their first dental check as soon as possible – there's no need to wait until all the teeth are through. Parents should begin brushing their children's teeth as soon as they appear and should keep doing this until the child is at least 7 years old and can manage alone. For more information, contact the *British Dental Health Foundation's Word of Mouth helpline on 0645 551188.*

Home treatment

If your teeth are sensitive, use a special 'desensitising' toothpaste. For toothache, take simple painkillers (use sugar free products for babies and young children) and see your dentist.

> **See your dentist if:**
> - You have toothache
> - Bleeding and painful gums keep occurring even with regular brushing and flossing
> - You experience pain wearing dentures
> - You develop a dry mouth
> - You have a mouth ulcer present for longer than 2 weeks
>
> If you have trouble finding an NHS dentist, contact your local health authority (number in phone book or the *Health Information Service* (p59).

 ➡ Useful contacts – p60

HEADACHE AND MIGRAINE

Headaches are very common and most have no serious cause. Occasionally, headaches are due to a serious illness, so it is important to know when to go to your doctor (see 'Consult your doctor if' below). Most headaches soon pass, and are easily treated with simple painkillers.

Signs and symptoms

'Headache' describes a number of different pains. Other symptoms may also be present,

including:

- Neck pain, spreading over the top of the head
- Pain in one spot or on one side of the head
- Pain behind the eyes or at the front of the head
- Nausea and vomiting (with bad headache)
- Sight may be affected.

Causes and complications

Stress, tension and tiredness are some of the most common causes of headaches. Other causes are:

- Dental problems, including grinding your teeth while you sleep
- 'Hangovers' and dehydration
- Infections causing fever, colds or flu etc.
- Joint and bone problems of the neck
- Poor posture
- Fumes from badly ventilated fires
- Migraine
- A blow to the head.

Everyday headaches make you irritable and decrease your concentration, which can cause accidents at home, work and while driving. **It's important not to overdose on painkillers,** especially paracetamol - keep to the correct dose noted on the label.

Prevention

Because headaches have different causes, there are many different ways to prevent them.

- Take time out to relax if you feel tense.
- See your dentist if you think you have a problem with your teeth.
- Don't drink too much alcohol (p12). After taking alcohol, drink at least two large glasses of water before going to bed and the same again in the morning.
- Eat regular meals, including a good breakfast.
- Get enough sleep (p13).

- Make sure you have enough fresh air, especially if there is an open or gas fire (poorly maintained gas appliances can cause carbon monoxide poisoning)
- If you get migraine, avoid the causes (see Migraine, below).

Home treatment

- Take simple painkillers like paracetamol, ibuprofen or soluble aspirin (aspirin only in people over 12 years).
- Try to relax and avoid stress.
- Place a cool cloth on the forehead.
- Arrange to have your sight tested by an ophthalmic optician (optometrist).

Consult your doctor if:

- You develop a sudden, blinding headache, and you lose strength in your legs and arms
- It's the first headache you've had that does not get better after 3 days of home treatment.
- Light hurts your eyes or there are problems with your sight
- There are signs of meningitis (see p47)
- A headache develops a few hours or days after a head injury
- Seek urgent medical attention if you suspect carbon monoxide poisoning.

Migraine

Migraine is a type of severe headache that runs in families and can be brought on by certain foods, e.g. red wine, blue cheeses and chocolate. Other factors like stress, the weather and hormone changes can also cause a migraine. Often, problems with vision - e.g. bright lights or chequer-board patterns - occur before the headache begins. A migraine can last from a few minutes to several days.
Home treatment: During a migraine, the eyes are often sensitive to light, and lying in a darkened room can help. However, nowadays migraine sufferers are encouraged to try to get on with 'normal' life even during an attack. Ibuprofen or paracetamol may help ease the pain. The *Migraine Action Association*, p60, will provide you with more information and support.
Consult your doctor if: Your home treatment doesn't work. Your doctor may decide to prescribe other migraine treatments suitable for you.

➡ **Alcohol and your health - p12**
➡ **Good sleeping habits - p13**

➡ **Meningitis - p47**
➡ **Useful contacts - p60**

MUSCLE AND JOINT PAIN

- Long-term inflammation (e.g. due to arthritis)
- Inflammation of the soft tissue around a joint
- Formation of uric acid crystals in the joint (called gout)
- Wear and tear on the internal surfaces of the joint (called osteoarthritis)

A minor joint injury can cause stiffness and stop you using it properly. This may in turn affect the joint's ability to move (e.g. frozen shoulder)

Home treatment

- For muscle pain, massage the area and keep it warm. Warm baths and rest are helpful. Take simple painkillers like paracetamol or ibuprofen, which helps reduce inflammation.
- For how to treat sprains and strains, see p9.
- For other types of joint pain, rest the sore joint and take painkillers like paracetamol, aspirin (not in children under 12 years) or ibuprofen.

Muscle and joint pains are common and seldom need the attention of a doctor. In most cases, the problem will get better on its own, and a few steps can help reduce the pain in the meantime.

Signs and symptoms

Pain and stiffness in a muscle or joint, especially when you move.
Pain, swelling and bruising of a joint, which may also feel hot.

Causes and complications

In most cases, muscle pain results from a strain due to over-exertion.
Joint pain can be caused by several things:
An injury, such as a sprain or strain
Temporary inflammation (e.g. due to a viral infection)

> ### Consult your doctor if:
> - The joint or muscle pain does not improve after 3 days
> - The joint looks deformed
> - One of your joints is painful, hot and swollen
> - The joint keeps getting stiffer and less able to move.

Tennis elbow

This is a common injury that can be caused by any activity that uses the arm a lot. The muscles and ligaments around the elbow joint become strained, and cause the elbow pain. The whole arm

may also be painful.
Home treatment: Rest the elbow for 2-3 weeks and support the arm in a sling or put an elastic bandage around the elbow.
Consult your doctor if: The problem continues after 2-3 weeks of rest and support.

➡ **Sprains and strains - p9**

COLDS AND FLU

Colds and flu (influenza) are often confused. Their symptoms are similar but colds are more common and usually less serious. Flu also tends to last longer, and can leave you feeling under the weather for two or more weeks. Antibiotics have no effect on uncomplicated colds or flu, but simple home treatments can help you feel better.

Signs and symptoms

- **Colds:** Mild fever, runny nose and sneezing, watery eyes, cough and sore throat.
- **Flu:** Fever, chills and high temperature, headache, muscle and bone aches, and dry cough. Runny nose and sneezing may also occur.
- Chesty cough and earache can occur, if there is a chest or ear infection.

Causes and complications

Colds and flu are caused by viruses. There are many different types of these viruses which is why you can catch them more than once. They are passed between people in mucus droplets from sneezing or coughing, or by physical contact (e.g. unwashed hands).

Colds are seldom serious but can cause problems in babies, the very old, and those with serious illness. Bacterial infections of the ears (see p41) and chest can be a problem in both conditions, but especially with flu.

Prevention

It's difficult to prevent yourself catching colds and flu, but you can cut down your chances by keeping away from infected people. If you fall into the list of those who are in danger of getting seriously ill from flu ask your doctor about a flu vaccination (see 'When a flu vaccination is needed', p23). A balanced diet and regular activity (p11-12) will help boost your immune system and your resistance to colds and flu.

Home treatment

There is no cure for colds and flu. Antibiotics are of no use, unless you get a chest or ear infection as well. Following a few simple steps will help you feel better and get well faster:

- Rest - don't exercise
- Drink plenty of non-alcoholic fluids. Fluids are especially important for children to replace water they lose through sweating
- Take paracetamol, ibuprofen or soluble aspirin, but follow the instructions on the label. Children under 12 years can be given a sugar free paracetamol syrup
- Stop smoking (see p10)
- Keep your bedroom warm but airy - don't wrap children up too warmly
- Sponge children with lukewarm water if their temperature is high (see p47)
- Stay at home for a couple of days after the symptoms are gone.

For further tips on how to treat common symptoms of colds and flu, see 'Catarrh and sinusitis,' p23, 'Coughs' and 'Sore throats', p27

Consult your doctor if:

- The fever is still there after 4 days
- Fluid intake has declined or stopped
- A child acts oddly, e.g. change in speaking or walking, unable to sit up, drowsy all the time
- There is any wheezing with breathing
- There is very bad earache (see p41)
- There are signs of meningitis (see p47)
- There is chest pain or shortness of breath.

When a flu vaccination is needed
Flu vaccination reduces a person's risk of catching flu by up to about 70-80%. A new vaccination is needed every year. People who may need a flu vaccination include those with:
■ Chest disorders like bronchitis, asthma, emphysema or cystic fibrosis
■ A long-term heart disorder

■ Diabetes
■ Kidney disease
■ Poor resistance to infections or any other serious illnesses - ask your doctor if you're unsure.
Also, anyone living in a nursing home, residential home or long-stay facility for the elderly may need a vaccination.

Catarrh and sinusitis

Catarrh and sinusitis may cause watery mucus from the nose that turns green over a few days, loss of smell and taste, throat irritation and coughing, and facial pain, especially when you bend forward. Catarrh and sinusitis often occur when you have a cold or flu, but can also be due to an allergic reaction like hay fever. These problems are not generally serious.
Home treatment: Don't smoke and keep away from smoky or very dry areas. Blow your nose gently (clear one nostril at a time). Steam inhalation (e.g. with menthol crystals) will help (see p57). Ask your pharmacist about decongestant nasal drops or a spray, as well as painkillers, if you think you need them.
Consult your doctor if: The pain of sinusitis continues, especially when you cough or bend forward. If you have a high temperature (over 39°C/102F, see p47), or there are any signs of meningitis (see p47).

➡️**Ear problems - p41**   ➡️**Home Medicine Chest - p57**
➡️**Fevers - p47**   ➡️**Meningitis - p47**

COUGHS

Coughing is the body's way of getting mucus and dust out of the lungs, so it is an important process. Coughing occurs when the windpipe is irritated by something, but if there is nothing to clear from the lungs, it is just a nuisance.

Signs and symptoms
Symptoms can also include an itchy or sore throat, or painful chest muscles. You may cough up some mucus and phlegm (a 'chesty' cough), although this does not always happen ('dry' cough).

Causes and complications
■ Infection of the airway and chest caused by viruses or bacteria
■ Blocked nose and catarrh
■ Irritation due to allergies (e.g. asthma)
■ Smoking or smoke
■ Dry or dusty atmosphere.
Bad coughing that lasts a long time can cause vomiting, and if the cough is very violent, spots of blood sometimes appear in the saliva and phlegm.

Prevention
If you have a cough, don't smoke. You can also try to keep out of smoky or dusty areas, and make sure the air is humid enough (e.g. place a damp towel over the back of a chair).

Home treatment

Steam inhalation will help (see p57). Suck lozenges (preferably sugar free, and keep to the recommended dose) and take warm drinks like a teaspoon each of honey and lemon dissolved in warm water to soothe your throat. You can try cough medicine from your pharmacist made for the type of cough you have, e.g. 'dry' or 'chesty'.

Consult your doctor if:
- Coughing is painful or lasts more than 5 days
- There is blood in your phlegm
- You are short of breath
- You are losing weight unexpectedly.

➡**Home Medicine Chest - p57**
➡**Catarrh and sinusitis - p23**

HAY FEVER

Hay fever (also known as allergic rhinitis) is a common allergic reaction that affects the eyes and the lining of the nose (see p26).

Signs and symptoms

Hay fever causes a number of symptoms, and these are usually worst in the late spring and autumn. Symptoms include:
- Sneezing, often very hard and lasting a long time
- Watery and inflamed eyes
- Poor sense of smell and taste
- Wheezing
- Dry cough.

Causes and complications

Hay fever is usually brought on by pollen from grass, flowers and trees. However, symptoms can also be caused by other substances like pet hairs and dust mite droppings. Hay fever is not a serious problem, but if you suffer from a chest problem like asthma it can make you feel much worse.

Prevention

You can help your hayfever by:
- Stopping smoking
- Not stroking pets
- Keeping away from pollen: visit the seaside on holiday rather than the countryside, and keep your car windows closed when driving in the country
- Fitting a pollen filter to your vacuum cleaner; follow the manufacturer's instructions
- Checking the pollen count: if it's above 50 grains per cubic metre, be extra careful, and watch out for rises in the pollen levels in the middle of the morning and early evening. During spring and summer, radio and TV weather forecasts often give information on pollen counts.

Home treatment

You can get hay fever remedies from your pharmacist. These include antihistamine tablets (ask for those that don't cause drowsiness if you're driving or operating heavy machinery), nasal sprays and eye drops. Take your tablets in the morning, before the symptoms start, and, if you find they help, carry your nasal sprays and eye drops with you, to use if the pollen count starts to go up.

> **Consult your doctor if:**
> - If you are getting breathless or are wheezing heavily
> - You suffer from asthma and are having difficulty breathing, even when you use an inhaler

 ➡ **Home Medicine Chest - p57**
➡ **Catarrh and sinusitis - p23**

SORE THROATS AND TONSILLITIS

Sore throats are common and seldom serious. Most sore throats will settle within a few days without needing any medication. Laryngitis, which is an infection of the voice box, can also cause a sore throat.

Tonsillitis simply means the tonsils are inflamed, and it is not usually serious. It's more common in children, who can get repeated attacks. Tonsils are an important part of the body's defence system, so they are rarely taken out nowadays. The discomfort of sore throats and tonsillitis can be helped by simple home remedies.

Signs and symptoms
- Throat and/or ear pain.
- Hoarseness or loss of voice.
- Swollen glands on either side of the neck or jaw.
- Difficulty with swallowing.

Causes and complications
Most sore throats are caused by viral infections. Tonsillitis can be due to infection by a virus or bacteria.
The most common problem is repeated tonsil infections, leading to a lot of time off school for children, and poor eating habits. Occasionally, tonsillitis can cause abscesses on the tonsils and the area around them (see 'Consult your doctor if', below).

Home treatment/Prevention

It is difficult to keep away from the germs that cause sore throats and tonsillitis. However, the discomfort can be soothed in the following ways:
- Gargle with soluble aspirin dissolved in a glass of water, and then swallow (not in children under 12 years). Drink warm liquids like honey (1 teaspoon) and lemon (1teaspoon) in warm water
- Don't drink acid drinks or eat spicy food
- Suck sugar free lozenges (read the label)
- Take simple painkillers (e.g. a sugar free liquid paracetamol preparation for children), especially at bed time.
- If you lose your voice from laryngitis, follow the tips above and try not to talk. Also, don't smoke or drink alcohol.

> **Consult your doctor if:**
> - Swallowing drinks is impossible
> - A child is drooling and seems unable to swallow their saliva
> - There are signs of meningitis (see p47)
> - There is difficulty breathing
> - There is a constant temperature over 39°C/102F (see p47)
> - There are repeated tonsil infections or abscesses.

 ➡ **Meningitis - p47**

ALLERGIES

An allergic reaction is when the body's defence system responds to a substance that doesn't affect most people. Allergies can be caused by many different substances and cause a wide range of symptoms. They can develop at anytime in life. Most allergies are unpleasant but not dangerous, although in a few people they can cause serious illness.

Signs and symptoms

Allergic reactions can affect the whole body or just the area of contact. The skin, airways and eyes are usually worst affected.
Symptoms may include:
- Sore, itchy, blotchy skin
- Chest tightness
- Shortness of breath
- Blocked or running nose, sneezing
- Eye irritation
- Long-term digestive problems
- Fluid retention
- Fatigue.

Causes and complications

Illness	Causes
Asthma (p27)	Dust, pet hairs, pollen, smoke
Hayfever (see p24)	Pollen, house dust mite droppings, pet hairs, mouldy dust
Eczema/ dermatitis (see p35)	Soap powders, nickel jewellery or watches, latex (e.g. rubber gloves), sticking plasters, hair dye, cosmetics, cement dust
Hives (see p36)	Nettles, strawberries, seafood (also called nettle rash or urticaria)
Coeliac disease	gluten (a protein found in wheat)

Certain foods or drugs can also cause an allergic reaction.

Anaphylactic shock is an extreme allergic reaction (see p7). **It's a medical emergency and you should phone 999 immediately**.

Prevention

The best way to deal with an allergy is to avoid the cause completely. If this is not possible, reduce your exposure as much as you can. The following steps may help:
- Wear hypoallergenic gloves (available from your pharmacy)
- Use a filter in the vacuum cleaner to remove dust mite droppings
- Wear protective clothing when handling material such as cement
- Wear a filter face mask in dusty areas
- Check food labels for substances causing allergies (e.g. peanut products)
- Use a barrier cream on exposed skin
- Try changing your clothes soap powder or fabric conditioner

Home treatment

- For skin rashes, bathe in a cool bath with a large spoonful of baking soda; apply calamine lotion to soothe the itching.
- For hayfever, use a nasal spray and eye drops (see p24).
- Use antihistamine cream, sprays or tablets for skin and hayfever symptoms
- Make sure you have medical supervision before starting any food exclusion diets (e.g. contact the *National Society for Research into Allergies,* p60).
- If you have ever had anaphylactic shock, you should always carry injectable adrenaline prescribed by your doctor.
- See your doctor if you have any new, unexpected or serious allergic reactions,or ask your pharmacist.

➡**Eczema - p35**
➡**Hayfever - p24**
➡**Hives - p36**
➡**Useful contacts - p60**

Asthma

Asthma is a condition that causes the airways to become inflamed and obstructed, so that breathing becomes difficult. It appears mostly in childhood but can also appear for the first time in adults. Many children grow out of asthma as they get older.

Signs and symptoms

- Breathlessness
- Wheezing (breathing with difficulty with a whistling sound)
- Coughing (often with mucus)
- Sweating and a fast pulse rate, if there is great difficulty breathing
- Coughing at night in children.

Causes and complications

Many different things can trigger asthma. It can be caused by an allergic reaction (e.g. a reaction to dust, smoke, mould, animal hair, certain food or drugs). Other causes can include over-exercise (doing too much too quickly), emotional upset, changes in weather, and colds or flu. Asthma is more common in children who are exposed to cigarette smoke at home. A severe attack of asthma can be dangerous if it's not controlled (see 'Consult your doctor if', below).

Prevention

- Try to identify the things that cause your asthma and avoid them.
- Avoid smoke of all kinds and stay indoors when air pollution is high.
- Keep your home as free of dust as possible, and avoid hairy pets, carpets and other soft furnishings.
- Do regular moderate activity (e.g. swimming). If exercise causes an asthma attack, talk to your doctor about it.
- Avoid aspirin, ibuprofen or cold and cough medicines unless your doctor tells you to take them.

Home treatment

Anyone who gets asthma for the first time, should see their doctor, who will be able to prescribe special medicines and inhaling devices to control your asthma. They will also teach you how to manage asthmatic attacks yourself and how to identify when to get help. If a child has an asthma attack, stay calm, give them their medication and help them relax. The *National Asthma Association,* p60, will also be able to provide more information and advice.

Consult your doctor if:

- You have asthma symptoms for the first time
- Your symptoms fail to respond to your usual treatment
- You begin to use your asthma medicine more often than usual
- You start producing a lot of phlegm that's green or bloody.

Call an ambulance (dial 999) or go immediately to the nearest Accident & Emergency department of the nearest hospital if you have a severe asthma attack and breathing is so difficult you feel like you're suffocating. In the meantime, take any medicine you might have to control your asthma. If one dose of an inhaler doesn't relieve the problem, repeat it once only.

 ➡ **Useful contacts - p60**

CONSTIPATION

Many people worry that they are constipated if they do not pass a motion every day, but this is not the case. What matters is if your normal pattern changes. If this happens, minor changes in your diet and exercise levels will usually solve the problem.

Signs and symptoms
- Bowel movements less often than usual, with irregular timing.
- Stools difficult to pass.
- Stomach pain and bloated feeling.

Causes and complications
Constipation can be caused by too little fluid intake, lack of fibre in the diet, too little physical activity, stress, pregnancy, over-use of laxatives and certain medicines (the label or leaflet that comes with a medicine will note whether constipation is likely to occur).

Constipation is rarely harmful, but you should not ignore warning signs of something more serious (see 'Consult your doctor if', below).

> ## Consult your doctor if:
> - After a few days you begin to vomit
> - You have severe abdominal pain
> - There is blood in your stool
> - You are losing weight unexpectedly
> - The change in bowel habit happened with no good reason (e.g. see 'Causes and complaints').

➡ **Wise eating - p12**
➡ **Physical activity - p13**

DIARRHOEA

Like vomiting, diarrhoea is a symptom of many different illnesses. It will usually settle on its own but it can be dangerous in small children and babies (see 'Diarrhoea in infants and children', p44).

Signs and symptoms
- Passing more than five loose and watery stools in 24 hours.
- Abdominal cramps may occur.
- Fever and vomiting may occur.

Causes and complications
Diarrhoea can be caused by food poisoning, a change in the bacteria in the bowel (e.g. after drinking water in foreign countries or taking antibiotics), drinking excess alcohol, stress, too much fat in the diet, irritation of the bowel by spicy foods, or a change of environment (e.g. when travelling on holiday). Occasionally, diarrhoea is caused by a serious underlying illness (see 'Consult your doctor if', below). A number of complications can result from diarrhoea:

Dehydration, especially in older people and the very young
Any existing illness may be made worse
Any medicines you are taking may not be properly absorbed
Severe irritation of the bottom.

Prevention

You can cut down your risk of getting diarrhoea by keeping high standards of hygiene (e.g. wash your hands before eating, or after going to the toilet). You can also:
Drink bottled water (or use purifying tablets) while abroad unless the water supply is pure, and avoid ice in drinks
Eat smaller meals more often
Drink alcohol in moderation
Wash and peel fruit
Only eat salads washed in pure water. Avoid them when abroad.

Home treatment

Drink plenty of non-sugary, non-alcoholic fluids - too much sugar can make diarrhoea worse.

- Babies and older people may need to replace lost salts and water by taking an oral rehydration solution (ORS), obtainable from your pharmacist. Anti-diarrhoeal medicines should only be used in babies and very old people under doctor's orders.
- Once the diarrhoea stops, try some solid food like grated apple or carrots, dry crackers, or lean meat. Avoid fatty foods.
- Wash your hands regularly, especially after going to the toilet, to avoid spreading any infection to others.

Consult your doctor if:
- You also have a high fever (see p46)
- You think you may have food poisoning
- The diarrhoea goes on for 3 days
- There is blood in the diarrhoea
- Phone your doctor if diarrhoea continues for more than 1 day in babies or 2 days in children under 12 years.

Incontinence

Urinary incontinence (leakage of urine) can occur with ageing, infection of the urinary system, increase in prostate size, and after childbirth. Bed wetting is common in children, and usually solves itself over time (see p43). Faecal incontinence (leakage of faeces) is caused by weakness of the muscle around the bottom, constipation (or excessive laxative use) and side effects of some medicines (e.g. some antibiotics).
Home treatment: Avoid late-night drinks and use the toilet at regular times during the day to feel more in control. Doing special exercises strengthens the muscles that control the passage of urine and stools. The self-help group *Continence Foundation* (p60) will be able to provide you with more information, while constipation is helped by dietary fibre, drinking fluids and taking regular physical activity (see p11-13).
Consult your doctor if: Incontinence seriously disrupts your lifestyle, if it suddenly happens and you can't identify any cause, or if you suspect urinary infection (see p50), or an enlarged prostate (see p55).

➡ **Bed wetting - p43**   ➡**Useful contacts - p60**
➡**Diarrhoea in children - p44**

INDIGESTION AND HEARTBURN

Indigestion is a general term for a number of symptoms that are caused when food is not properly digested or absorbed into the body. Although annoying, indigestion is usually harmless and can be easily prevented and treated.

Signs and symptoms
- Feeling of fullness.
- Vague pain/discomfort below the ribcage sometimes extending into the throat.
- A burning sensation in the chest/upper part of the abdomen, often called heartburn. This has nothing to do with a heart attack. (The symptoms of a heart attack are quite different, see p6).
- Sour taste in the mouth.
- Excessive wind and belching.
- Symptoms often worse at night.

Causes and complications
Indigestion usually occurs when the strong acid and digestive juices produced in the stomach cause inflammation of the lining of the stomach or intestine. Sometimes stomach acid also escapes upwards, into the gullet, causing 'heartburn'. Anyone can suffer from indigestion, although middle-aged people are most commonly affected, and it can be set off by rich, fatty food, irregular or rushed meals, alcohol and smoking.

Indigestion rarely leads to other problems, but repeated or long-lived attacks may indicate other illnesses like ulcers (see 'Consult your doctor if', below).

Prevention
- Try to identify the food and drink that causes your indigestion and don't take them.
- Avoid eating within an hour of going to bed.
- Eat small meals at regular intervals.
- Sleep with your upper body propped up with pillows.
- If you suffer from indigestion, try to avoid medicines that cause 'gastro-intestinal or gastro-duodenal' problems (read the labels), and ask your doctor or pharmacist about alternatives.

Home treatment

There are a number of medicines that treat indigestion. If you are confused about the best for you, ask your pharmacist for advice. Avoid taking sodium bicarbonate, unless you have checked with your doctor. Drink a glass of skimmed milk at bedtime, either to prevent indigestion, or to soothe it after the pain starts.

Consult your doctor if:
- Your indigestion is not helped by simple antacids or other non-prescription medicines
- Pain or cramps get worse after eating
- There is nausea or vomiting
- Your stools are very dark, or have blood in them
- You lose weight unexpectedly
- You are concerned it may be a heart problem.

➡ **Chest pain - p6**
➡ **Wise eating - p12**

➡ **Physical activity - p13**

Irritable bowel syndrome

Cramping pains in the lower abdomen, sometimes with constipation or diarrhoea, are often due to irritable bowel syndrome (IBS). The cause is not known, although stress, diet and lack of regular physical activity may be involved.

Prevention: Eat a high-fibre diet with whole grain bread, pasta, fresh fruit and vegetables (see p12). Try cutting out coffee, red meat and dairy products from your diet. Cutting down or stopping smoking, taking time to relax, and doing some exercise may also help (see p13).

Home treatment: Try putting a hot water bottle on the sore area. If you have severe pain, your doctor may prescribe an anti-spasmodic drug (also available from your pharmacist). Mild anti-diarrhoeal medicines or laxatives may help but must not be used long term.

Consult your doctor if: the home treatment doesn't work, there is blood in your stools or they are black or covered in mucus, or you lose weight unexpectedly.

PILES

Piles (also called haemorrhoids) are caused by the swelling of certain veins around the bottom. They can be very painful and annoying, but are rarely serious.

Signs and symptoms

Bleeding from the bottom (blood often found on the toilet paper).
Pain and tenderness around the bottom.
A soft lump, or purple grape-like lumps at the bottom (called external piles).
Pain on passing stools.

Causes and complications

Piles may be caused by straining at the toilet due to constipation, pregnancy, being overweight, standing for long periods, or lifting heavy weights. Associated problems can include:
Bleeding - this may not be dangerous
Blood clotting inside the piles, causing increased pain and making it difficult for external piles to return inside the bottom.
Constipation - don't avoid passing a stool because of the pain, as this will make it even more difficult later.

Prevention

Keep to a healthy weight (see p11), take plenty of regular activity like brisk walking, eat a high fibre diet (e.g. whole grain bread, pasta, vegetables and fruit) and drink plenty of fluids, especially fruit juices.

Home treatment

- Use soft toilet paper and go to the toilet when you feel you need to, don't put it off.
- Apply an ice pack to the piles.
- Try to gently push protruding piles back into the anus opening. Do this in a warm bath and use a lubricant.
- A bulking laxative may help - ask your pharmacist to recommend one.
- Gently smooth haemorrhoidal ointment on the piles to soothe and lubricate them - available from your pharmacist.

Consult your doctor if:

- You notice bleeding from the bottom
- The number of times you go to the toilet has changed, or you have occasional constipation and diarrhoea that keeps on happening
- You have lost weight unexpectedly
- You also have stomach pain

 ➡ **Eat well and stay trim - p11**

Vomiting

Vomiting is a very common symptom and rarely due to serious illness. Vomiting in children and babies is more dangerous because of the risk of dehydration (see 'Vomiting in infants and children', p48).

Signs and symptoms

Other signs may also occur with vomiting:
- a feeling of general illness before vomiting occurs (e.g. with food poisoning)
- stomach pain, especially after eating (e.g. due to a gut infection).

Causes and complications

Vomiting may occur because some food you have eaten is bad or because you have an infection of the gut. Other causes include migraine (see p20), pregnancy, ear infection (see p41), and also overeating and drinking too much alcohol (see p12). Repeated coughing will eventually lead to vomiting, especially in children (see p48). Very rarely, vomiting can be a sign of a more serious illness (see 'Consult your doctor if' below).

Home treatment

After a bout of vomiting, don't eat or drink anything for a few hours until your stomach has settled down. When you feel ready, take small sips of water, fruit juices diluted with lots of water (e.g. 1 part juice to 3 parts water), then move on to clear soup. Later, try dry toast or plain boiled rice (avoid milk and other dairy products, as well as meat and fatty foods as these may irritate the stomach). Take oral rehydration solution (ORS) to prevent the dehydration that can arise from vomiting or diarrhoea. These are available from your pharmacist, as are anti-emetics (anti-vomiting medicines) - check with your pharmacist that they are right for your problem.

Consult your doctor if:
- Vomiting goes on for over 24 hours, especially if you are pregnant
- You also have severe abdominal pain
- The vomit contains material that looks like soil or coffee grounds
- You also have a very bad headache
- The vomiting started after a bang on the head
- There is any blood in the vomit or your stools.

➡ **Healthy living - p10**
➡ **Ear infection - p41**
➡**Migraine - p20**
➡**Vomiting in children - p48**

Worms

Worms are very common, especially in children. You will actually see the worms in the stools, and the area around the bottom may be itchy, especially at night. Worms are usually caught from an infected person, and they spread quickly around families.

Prevention: Wash your hands after going to the toilet, after touching any animals, and especially before eating. If you keep pets, de-worm them regularly.

Home treatment: You can treat worms yourself with a medicine from your pharmacist (not in children under 2 years, unless your doctor says so). Remember to treat the whole family to prevent re-infection.

Consult your doctor if: You are uncertain about the symptoms, you have stomach bloating or pain, or if a pregnant woman or child with epilepsy gets worms.

TIREDNESS AND ANAEMIA

Everyone feels tired sometimes, usually because of too little sleep, but constant tiredness should be taken seriously. Anaemia, which is often due to a lack of iron, can cause tiredness as well as other symptoms, especially in women. Fortunately, it can be recognised and treated quite easily.

Signs and symptoms of anaemia

Skin, lips, tongue, nailbeds or the inside of eyelids are pale in colour.
Feeling of weakness.
Dizziness or fainting spells.
Breathlessness, especially after exercise.
Fast heartbeat felt in the neck or chest (palpitations).

Causes and complications

The usual cause of anaemia is lack of iron in the diet and sometimes lack of vitamin B12. It can also occur after blood loss (e.g. frequent nose bleeds, heavy periods) or during pregnancy. Tiredness due to anaemia or any of the other causes described below increases the risk of accidents, interferes with work, and puts a strain on personal and family relationships.

Home treatment

If anaemia is confirmed by a blood test, your doctor may prescribe iron tablets. You can also help yourself by eating plenty of iron-rich foods like dried fruit and leafy vegetables, and by drinking orange juice with meals.

Dealing with other causes of tiredness

- **Disturbed sleep:** Try getting one or two uninterrupted nights and see if you feel better (see p13).
- **Depression and stress:** The tiredness associated with these conditions should improve if the underlying problem is treated appropriately (see p13).
- **Excess alcohol intake:** Even if you drink only moderately, try cutting out all alcohol for a week or so (see p12).
- **Recent infectious illness:** Don't expect too much of yourself after an illness like flu. Eat a nourishing diet and take things easy for a couple of weeks.

Consult your doctor if:

- The problem continues after you have tried the actions listed above
- You are constantly tired for no apparent reason - especially if it's affecting your work or relationships
- You have difficulty sleeping because of night-time trips to the toilet
- Your stools are black and tar-like.

 ➡ **Healthy living - p10**

ACNE

Acne, or pimples, is a complaint that affects many people. It's most common in teenagers but can occur at any age. Most cases are mild and can be treated at home. In very bad cases, early diagnosis and treatment by your doctor will minimise the distress it causes and reduce the risk of permanent scarring.

Signs and symptoms

- Painful raised red spots that may be pus-filled.
- Painless raised white or black spots (white-heads/blackheads).
- Spots usually on the face, but also on the scalp, neck, back and upper chest.

Causes and complications

The cause is not completely understood but hormone changes, certain medicines and oily cosmetics may have a role to play.

Following some simple guidelines will reduce the severity of acne and the risk of scarring.

- Clean your skin with a mild medicated soap or soap-free cleanser (without alcohol).
- Don't squeeze, pick or prick spots, as this can cause scarring.
- If you use cosmetics, choose water-based not oil-based products.
- Apply anti-acne cream - available from your pharmacist.
- Contact the *Acne Support Group*, p60, for more information and support.

> **Consult your doctor if:**
> - The acne is severe and you are embarrassed about it.

 ➡ **Useful contacts - p60**

ATHLETE'S FOOT

Athlete's foot is a common skin problem caused by a fungal infection that can affect anyone. It can be easily treated without seeing your doctor.

Signs and symptoms

- Sore, itchy and broken skin between the toes and on the sole of the foot.
- Bleeding when scratching the foot.
- Smelly feet.

Causes

The fungus causing athlete's foot grows well in warm, damp areas, and can be picked up from swimming pools, baths, shared towels or even wet floors.

Prevention

- Wash your feet at least once a day, or more often if they are dirty.
- Dry thoroughly, especially between the toes.

- Wear clean wool or cotton socks.
- Never wear trainers without socks on.
- Avoid walking barefoot on soil or damp floors.
- When possible expose your feet to the air and wear sandals without socks.

You can treat athlete's foot at home. Apply an antifungal cream or powder - available from your pharmacist. Keep using the treatment until your feet have been free of the fungus for at least 2 weeks.

> **Consult your doctor if:**
> - Your toenails become black or discoloured.

COLD SORES

Cold sores are crops of painful blisters that usually appear on the face. They often keep reappearing. Cold sores eventually heal on their own, but you can do a lot to help relieve the discomfort.

Signs and symptoms

- Small blisters around the lips (most common), nose and other parts of the face.
- Pain and a burning/tingling sensation is usually felt just before the rash appears.
- The blisters crust over and heal in about 8-10 days.

Causes and complications

Cold sores are caused by a virus infection. Once you have the infection, it stays in the skin and can cause cold sores later on, especially either after sun exposure or when you have another illness or are under stress. Cold sores are very infectious and they are spread by contact between people. The main danger with cold sores is where blisters form in or near the eye - you must see your doctor if this happens. Cold sores are also related to genital herpes which is transmitted during sexual intercourse or oral sex.

Home treatment/Prevention

Don't kiss people who have cold sores on the mouth. If you get cold sores, avoid sudden changes in temperature and the sun. If you feel the tingling that happens before an outbreak, apply a cream for cold sores (from your pharmacist) to prevent the sore developing or at least reduce its severity.

If you have an outbreak of cold sores, take simple painkillers if necessary. Use a lip salve before going into sunlight and, if possible, cover your mouth with a scarf. Don't scratch and break the blisters. Use your own towel.

Consult your doctor if:
- The outbreak of blisters occurs near your eye or at the tip of your nose.
- You also have a sore red eye.
- The sores do not heal in 10 days.
- You also suffer from a serious illness or develop a high temperature (see p47).

ECZEMA AND DERMATITIS

Eczema is a form of dermatitis, which means inflammation of the skin. It's not infectious, and rarely serious. The most common type, known as 'atopic eczema', is an allergic reaction that usually appears for the first time in babies (see p45) and is often accompanied by asthma or hay fever. Other types of eczema include 'contact dermatitis', which is caused by contact with a substance to which you're allergic.

You can do a lot to prevent or control eczema, although in very bad cases you may need powerful medicines from your doctor.

Signs and symptoms
- A cluster of blisters that may be crusty or weeping.
- Red, dry, cracked or flaking, scaly skin, which often gets worse in cold conditions.
- Itching.
- Eczema and dermatitis can occur anywhere on the body, but eczema is most common on the insides of elbows and knees; 'contact dermatitis' often occurs on the hands.
- 'Seborrhoeic dermatitis' usually affects the nose, scalp and hairy parts of the face or chest. It's often flaky and red, but in severe cases it can produce a thick, yellow, greasy scale on the scalp and eyebrows. **Dandruff** may also result.

Causes and complications

Eczema is an allergic reaction causing inflammation of the skin. Sometimes the cause is unknown, but 'contact dermatitis' can result from contact with cosmetics, detergents, hair dye, nickel watches and cheap jewellery, or a substance that irritates your skin like cement dust. If it's not treated, eczema and dermatitis can become infected.

Prevention

Identify and avoid substances, materials or chemicals that set off your eczema. Wear protective gloves when using household detergents, and use protective gloves and clothing if you have to handle industrial chemicals or cement.

Help prevent dry skin by using moisturising creams and bath oils. Contact the *National Eczema Society* for further guidance (see p60).

Home treatment

- Use creams and lotions obtainable from your pharmacist to stop the itchiness and keep your skin moist.
- Avoid scratching.
- Simple antihistamines may help to control itching. Ask your pharmacist for those that don't cause drowsiness if you're driving.
- You can obtain a low strength steroid cream from your pharmacist, but be sure to follow the instructions carefully. **Ask your doctor before using steroids in children.**

Consult your doctor if:

- Your symptoms are very painful, or you think your skin is infected
- The eczema is spreading very quickly
- You catch chicken pox (see p43)
- You have a temperature
- It may be an allergy

(i) ➡ **Allergies - p26**
   ➡ **Cradle cap - p45**

➡ **Eczema in children - p45**
➡ **Useful contacts - p60**

Hives

Hives (also called urticaria or nettle rash) is a rash from an allergic reaction to certain foods (e.g. shellfish, strawberries), medicines, plants (e.g. nettles), extreme heat and cold, or flea bites. The rash is made up of bright red, slightly raised spots or patches with pale centres.
Home treatment: The rash will usually disappear in a few hours on its own. However, you might like to try an antihistamine cream available from your pharmacist, or smooth on a soothing lotion like calamine.
Consult your doctor if: There are repeated attacks or the rash lasts more than 24 hours, even after applying an antihistamine cream. **Get urgent medical attention if your face and mouth begin to swell.**

Impetigo

Impetigo is a bacterial infection of the skin. It's most common in children, although adults can also get it. It's very infectious. Impetigo usually occurs on the face, especially around the corners of the mouth, although other parts of the body can be affected.

Home treatment and Prevention: Avoid direct contact with any infected people and use separate face flannels, towels and shaving equipment. Special shampoos and gels are available from your pharmacist.
Consult your doctor if: Your impetigo does not clear up after 3 days of using products from your pharmacist.

LICE

Lice are tiny parasitic insects that can live on the hairy parts of the body, where they suck blood from the skin. They prefer clean people. Head lice are very common amongst children and all lice are easily passed between people, so parents, teachers and grandparents often catch them. Lice are generally harmless, and can be treated at home.

Signs and symptoms

- Itchiness, constant scratching.
- Redness or rash on the skin.
- White specks (the nits or eggs) attached to the hair shafts.

Lice usually affect the scalp (head lice), body (body lice) and pubic areas (crab lice). Crab lice can also infect the eyebrows.

Causes and complications

Lice are caught from other people's heads and bodies, their clothes, bedding, chair backs, combs etc. (but not from animals). Female lice lay eggs every day, which take 8-10 days to hatch. So, you need to remove all the adults and all the eggs. Lice rarely cause serious harm, although excessive scratching can lead to skin infection.

Prevention

Don't share hats, scarves and combs with someone who has lice. If one family member has lice, check and treat everyone together to prevent being re-infected. Also, disinfect combs, brushes etc. by soaking them in antiseptic solutions. Wash all towels, clothes, bedding etc. in hot soapy water and use a hot iron to kill nits. Have hats, caps, jackets etc. dry cleaned.

Home treatment

- Ask your local practice (surgery) nurse, school nurse or health visitor, or your pharmacist about an appropriate shampoo or lotion (for either hair, body or pubic lice). Follow the instructions on the label carefully. This will kill the adult lice but not the eggs. Repeat after 24 hours, dry the hair, and then use a fine-toothed 'nit' comb (available from your pharmacist) to remove all dead lice and eggs. The *Community Hygiene Concern* (p60) will also be able to provide you with extra information on how to deal with the problem while your local *NHS Sexual Health* (GUM) *Clinic* (p61) will be able to inform you about pubic lice.
- Keep the hair clean, apply a conditioner and comb the hair daily with a 'nit' comb. This will help remove any remaining eggs.
- Many treatments for lice contain powerful chemicals that may be harmful to young children if used too often. If in doubt, ask your pharmacist for advice, and use the conditioner and nit comb method only.

Consult your doctor if:
- The home treatment is not working
- An infection develops, with fever, boils on the skin or a pus discharge.

 ➡Useful contacts - p60

Moles

Most moles are harmless but sudden changes in the way they look can occasionally be a sign of skin cancer. Caught early, most skin cancers can be removed, so see your doctor immediately if you notice:

- Any mole that changes shape or colour, or starts to bleed
- Lumps on the lower lip, forehead or tip of the ear
- Scaly or scabbed patches that don't heal.

PSORIASIS

Psoriasis is a skin disorder that usually occurs for the first time in young adults, and may last a lifetime. It's not infectious. There is no cure, but it can be controlled by remedies available from your pharmacist, although your doctor can provide additional treatment if required.

Signs and symptoms

- Red raised patches on the skin, with white or silvery scales.
- Usually affects thicker skin, such as the elbows, knees and hands/nails. It also affects the scalp, eyebrows and buttocks, although any part can be involved.
- Slight itch.
- Pitted nails, or loose nails.

Causes and complications

The cause of psoriasis is not fully understood, but it is known to run in families and is made worse by stress. Psoriasis can cause depression. It's important not to scratch psoriasis as this can cause infection.

Home treatment

You can't cure psoriasis, but you can limit its severity by:

- Applying moisturising creams and lotions, and avoiding strong soaps - and don't scratch
- Exposing the affected areas to sunlight for about 15-30 minutes in the morning or evening - don't overdo it (see 'Protect against the sun', p13)
- Applying cream or ointment recommended by your pharmacist or doctor.

Psoriasis can be very distressing, but self-help groups like the *Psoriasis Association* (p60) can help you cope.

Consult your doctor if:

- You develop scaly skin patches for the first time and think you may have psoriasis
- The condition is not controlled by the remedies described above or the skin patches become infected or painful
- Your joints become painful and inflamed.

➡ **Useful contacts - p60**
➡ **Protect against the sun - p13**

RINGWORM

Ringworm is a fungal infection. It can affect any part of the skin, but commonly occurs on the scalp, nails, armpit and groin. It's easily treated at home.

Signs and symptoms

- Ring-shaped patches of red, scaly, itchy skin.
- Inflammation and bleeding of the skin, due to scratching.
- Bald patches on the scalp.
- Thickening of the nail and tissues under the nail.

Causes and complications

Ringworm should be treated as soon as possible. If not treated, ringworm can lead to hair loss, skin infection or deformed nails.

Prevention

Ringworm is infectious, so avoid using the same towel or face flannel as someone with the condition.

Home treatment

Use an antifungal cream, powder or shampoo - available from your pharmacist. Don't scratch the area and keep it dry. Expose the affected area to air as much as possible.

Consult your doctor if:

- Symptoms do not improve with antifungal cream or powder
- The affected skin becomes infected and crusty
- Your nails are affected
- You develop bald patches on the scalp
- You have some other illness as well, or develop a high temperature.

Scabies

Scabies is caused by a mite that burrows into the skin to lay its eggs. It can be passed from person to person. Scabies is not serious, although it causes itchy red bumps on the skin (especially the hands, wrists, underside of elbows, genitals and other body creases). Scabs and sores may develop due to scratching. The itch is usually worse at night.

Home treatment: Ointments are available from your pharmacist. Follow the directions on the label or leaflet carefully. You will need to cover the whole body with ointment for 24 hours. Also, wash your clothing and bedding in hot soapy water.

Consult your doctor: if these steps do not cure the problem. The *Community Hygiene Concern*, p60, will be able to give you with information.

➡ **Useful contacts - p60**

SHINGLES

Shingles is a painful skin rash that usually affects the elderly or the weak (e.g. it often affects people during illness). Shingles is not usually serious, and can be treated at home in most cases.

Signs and symptoms

A painful rash, usually occurring on a narrow strip of skin on one side of the body - often on the chest wall, face and upper legs. A tingling itch usually occurs before the rash. There is often also flu-like illness, which may continue after the rash has gone.

Causes and complications

Shingles is caused by a virus infection. This is the same virus that causes chicken pox, so there is a very small risk of catching chicken pox (p43) from someone with shingles (but you can't catch shingles from someone with chicken pox). Problems are more likely in people whose resistance to illness is reduced for any reason. If it appears on the face, shingles can damage the eyes.

Home treatment/Prevention

Take simple painkillers like soluble aspirin (not in children under 12 years), paracetamol or ibuprofen. Keep the rash area uncovered as much as possible and try not to scratch it. Soothe the itch with calamine lotion. If there is pain after the rash has gone, cool the area with a bag of ice.

Consult your doctor if:
- The rash appears on your face
- You are suffering from some other illness or you are taking medicine that reduces your ability to fight infection
- The rash continues after 3-4 weeks
- You develop shingles more than once within 4-6 weeks.

WARTS AND VERRUCAS

Warts and verrucas (warts on the sole of your foot) are very common, and are not due to poor hygiene. They can grow anywhere on the skin, and are slightly infectious. You can treat warts and verrucas with products from your pharmacist. Your doctor can also remove them using various methods.

Signs and symptoms
- Cauliflower-like skin growth with a rough surface (verrucas are flat because they get walked on).
- Warts can grow anywhere, although they are common on the hands. Genital warts are softer and paler then warts elsewhere.
- Verrucas occur on the sole of the foot and can be painful when walking.

Causes and complications

Warts and verrucas are caused by a virus that invades skin cells, making them multiply and form an outgrowth. Warts can spread to different areas of the body. The virus is not very infectious, but it can be caught from contact with other infected people, or from wet floors (e.g. in public swimming pools). Warts are not usually serious, but genital warts may increase the risk of cervical cancer. So, if you think you have this type of wart, be sure to visit your doctor or sexual health (GUM/STD) clinic for diagnosis and treatment. Other warts are often best left alone, as most of them disappear naturally in time.

Prevention

Although warts are not very infectious, don't use the same face flannel and towels as people who have warts or verrucas. It's advisable to wear verruca socks while swimming. If you have genital warts, you must tell your sexual partner so they can seek medical advice.

Home treatment

Apply wart cream, paint or lotion, available from your pharmacist. These must be used every day for at least 3 weeks in order to work. Some of the lotions attack any skin, so protect normal skin by applying the lotion to the wart or verruca after cutting a hole in an adhesive plaster and using it to protect the surrounding skin After treatment, remove the dead skin by rubbing it with a pumice stone.

Consult your doctor if:
- You have genital warts
- You are diabetic and have verruca - foot care is important in diabetics
- There is any possibility that the 'wart' might be a mole that is getting larger, bleeding, changing colour or becoming itchy (see p38).

➡ **Moles - p38**

EAR PROBLEMS

Most ear problems are unlikely to cause permanent loss of hearing and can be dealt with at home. But remember that repeated exposure to very loud noise (e.g. from a personal stereo) can slowly cause a long-lasting loss of hearing.

Recognising common ear problems

- **Cold exposure** may result in a mild earache.
- **An insect or foreign body** causes buzzing or hissing in the ear, and a tickling sensation.
- **Ear infection** can be caused by bacteria or viruses. A **middle ear infection** results in severe earache, poor hearing, fever, and sometimes a greenish-yellow discharge. It is very important to treat middle ear infection. If untreated, the infection can lead to hearing loss. An outer ear infection causes painful earache that worsens when you pull at the ear lobe, itchy cracks in the ear canal, and discharge.
- **Wax blockage** can cause earache, a blocked feeling, and hearing loss.

Home treatment

Mild earache can be treated by taking the recommended dose of soluble aspirin (not in children under 12 years) or paracetamol. Placing a covered hot water bottle against the ear may also help. Infections may also need antibiotic drops from your doctor - you should always consult your doctor about a continuing pain in the ear (see 'Consult your doctor if').
Ear wax should be softened for up to 5 days using drops from your pharmacist.

Prevention

Try to reduce your exposure to very loud noises. If there are loud noises in your work place, wear ear defenders (ask your employer to supply a pair, if relevant). Also, try not to expose yourself to too much very loud noise out of work - e.g. at a rock concert, you could try wearing ear plugs. If you use a personal stereo, play it at a reasonable level. Never poke any objects into the ear (e.g. cotton buds), they can cause infection and your ear to produce excess earwax.

Consult your doctor if:

- You have constant ringing, buzzing or hissing in the ears
- There is severe pain, or pain that lasts longer than 24 hours
- You experience rapid, noticeable hearing loss
- There is discharge from the ears
- You suspect a middle ear infection
- After softening wax with drops for a maximum of 5 days, your ears are still full of wax.

 ➔ **Useful contacts - p60**

EYE PROBLEMS

Eye symptoms such as irritation and redness are common but they are rarely serious. It's important, however, to recognise the signs of potentially serious conditions that require immediate medical attention.

Recognising common eye conditions

- **Conjunctivitis** results in watering and bloodshot eyes with sticky discharge, gritty sensation and dislike of bright lights.
- **Dry eye** is recognised by bloodshot eyes, with a gritty feeling. There is no watering, as too few tears are produced. Infection is more likely.
- **Eye irritation** causes watering and bloodshot eyes as a result of external irritation; e.g. exposure to chemical fumes.
- **A foreign body** (e.g. grit) in the eye or stuck under the eyelid gives a painful and uncomfortable gritty sensation, causing red, watering eyes that may be difficult to open. If the particle is not removed, it can cause serious damage to the eye.
- **Stye** is a red lump on the eyelid. It may itch or cause slight pain or discomfort on the eyelid where the lashes are. It's due to a boil at the base of an eyelash caused by bacterial infection.

Home treatment

For **minor eye irritation and conjunctivitis**, try bathing gently with warm water every hour. Use a separate piece of cotton wool each time you wipe the eye. Drops and ointments from your pharmacist can be used to treat **conjunctivitis and styes**. For **dry eye**, your pharmacist can advise on lubricating eye drops in the first instance, but if it continues, see your doctor.

Foreign bodies can usually be removed by flushing the eye with water under a running tap or, if you can see the particle, removing it gently with the corner of a clean handkerchief.

Remember, don't wear any type of contact lens if you have an eye infection, and don't rub irritated and sore eyes, it may make matters worse.

Contact the *Eye Care Information Service* for more information, p60.

Prevention

You can reduce your risk of minor eye problems by avoiding exposure to irritants and wearing protective goggles if you are doing tasks that may produce airborne particles or dust (e.g. DIY). If someone in the household has an eye infection, make sure everyone uses separate face flannels and towels to avoid spreading the infection. It is worthwhile having your sight tested every two years, or more frequently if your optometrist recommends it. And, if you wear contact lenses, follow the instructions for cleaning them carefully.

Consult your doctor if:

- You have any kind of eye injury
- There is a deep pain in or at the back of the eye
- Your vision is blurred and/or you see halos around lights
- There is a foreign body in the eye that can't be removed
- There is no improvement after 2 days of using drops from your pharmacist to treat an infection
- A newborn baby has sticky eyes with a pus discharge.

 ➡ Useful contacts - p60

COMMON INFANT AND CHILD ILLNESSES

Parents have an important role to play in keeping their children healthy, and helping them get better if they are ill by caring for them and reassuring them. Many of the minor ailments considered in this book may affect your child, but some are most common or occur only in children, and these are described in this section. If there is an illness that you can't find in this section, check the Index (p62-64) or Index of signs and symptoms (p16-17) to see where it occurs in the book. Every family with a child not yet at school, has a health visitor, who will also be able to give you help and advice.

Children usually need different amounts of medicines, or even different medicines, from adults. Always check the label, which will tell you if a medicine should be given to a baby or child, and how much should be given. *Never give aspirin to children under 12 years of age, unless you have checked with your doctor.* Keep all medicines out of reach of children.

BED WETTING

Bed wetting is common, even in 7 or 8 year old children. Bed wetting is usually not serious. Bed-wetting may start again at stressful times or during illness.

Home treatment

It is vital that parents don't get angry but rather reassure their children. Bedwetting is not a sign of laziness or naughtiness; children have very little control over their bedwetting and if they feel guilty, it will make things worse. Some psychologists suggest that you just wait for the problem to pass, but following the few simple tips given here should help in the meantime.
- Don't give the child drinks for at least an hour before bedtime.
- Make sure your child empties the bladder before going to bed.
- Put a potty close to the bed and leave a night light on.

- Set an alarm clock for 2-3 hours after your child falls asleep, so they wake up to go to the toilet (change the time each night by 10-20 minutes to stop them getting used to waking up at the same time).
- Keep a flannel-covered rubber sheet nearby so your child can put it over the wet sheets, and leave clean bedclothes next to the bed, so older children can change the bed themselves.
- Get a bed-wetting alarm. The alarms are best for children of 5 years and older, and you can borrow them from your health visitor.
- Teach your child 'control exercises' - e.g. counting to ten before releasing the flow of urine helps develop important muscles.

Contact your local school nurse, health visitor, or the organisation *ERIC* (see p61) for more information.

CHICKEN POX

Chicken pox is a relatively harmless illness that usually occurs in children. It is caused by a virus that is spread by sneezing, coughing, infected clothing and coming into contact with chicken pox blisters. Children who are exposed to the virus may develop chicken pox 1-3 weeks later. The chicken pox virus can remain dormant in the body and may cause shingles in later life, particularly at times of stress like ill health (see p39).

Signs and symptoms

A slight fever, stomach ache and general feeling of illness can occur a day or two before the rash. The rash is made up of flat, red spots that usually begin on the scalp, face and back. It can also spread to other parts of the body. The spots turn into very itchy, tiny blisters that then become cloudy, break open and form a crust. Fresh red spots are usually seen next to the blisters.

Prevention

Once your child has been in contact with an infected child there is little you can do to prevent chicken pox. It's very contagious, and the best you can do is to keep your child away from any other infected children.

Home treatment

- Use cool baths without soap every 3-4 hours for the first couple of days. Add a few tablespoons of sodium bicarbonate to the bath water.
- Antihistamines are available from your pharmacist. These help relieve the itching. Some of them cause sleepiness, so use them just before bed time. Calamine lotion also helps relieve the itching.
- Scratching can lead to infection and scarring - use cotton gloves or socks on your child's hand to stop scratching.
- Give paracetamol or ibuprofen to help reduce fever.

Consult your doctor if:

- Your child has suspected chicken pox and a serious illness or is taking steroids
- Sores appear in the eyes
- There is unexpected bruising
- There is a fever (see p46)
- The itching is severe.

DIARRHOEA IN INFANTS AND CHILDREN

It's common for babies, especially if they are breast fed, to have very soft faeces. However, if your baby does have diarrhoea, it's important to clear it up as quickly as possible, and to prevent dehydration.

Signs and symptoms

- Multiple loose stools.
- Unpleasant or different smell from normal.
- Thirstiness.
- Stomach cramps.

Causes and complications

Diarrhoea that suddenly happens in a healthy baby or young child is usually because of a change in diet. It can also result from a stomach infection, too much sugar, anxiety or excitement, and some medicines. Diarrhoea usually settles down on its own, but it can be dangerous in small children and babies if they lose too much water and become dehydrated. It can also cause a painful bottom, with inflammation around the anus.

Prevention

- Follow the directions for making up feeds, and sterilise all equipment.
- Don't give very sugary drinks or too much fat in the food.
- Wash your hands after changing your baby's nappy and before feeding.
- Use bottled water (or cooled boiled water) when abroad, and avoid salads and ice in drinks, unless the supply is pure.

Home treatment

- Stop giving solid food. Give cooled boiled water or other non-sugary fluids.
- Babies under 1 year may need to replace lost salts and water by taking an oral rehydration solution (ORS), available from your pharmacist. For bottle-fed babies, give the baby only ORS to drink for 24 hours. For breast-fed babies, increase the number of breast feeds and

give your baby ORS after each dirty nappy. If the baby won't take ORS from a bottle, use a teaspoon instead.

■ Slowly try more solid food (e.g. grated apple or carrots and lean meat). Don't give fatty foods and dairy products.

Consult your doctor if:

■ There is a high fever (p46)
■ There is blood in the diarrhoea
■ Your child or baby is drowsy, confused or vomiting repeatedly
■ Your child or baby refuses to drink or has signs of dehydration (e.g. sunken eyes, very little urine or stools passed, dry mouth, drowsiness and irritability, tight skin)
■ A child over 1 year has had diarrhoea for more than 2 days.

If you think a medicine is causing diarrhoea, consult your doctor or pharmacist, but don't just stop the medicine.

ECZEMA IN INFANTS AND CHILDREN

Eczema is common in babies, children and adults (see p35 for a description of the different types of eczema). Eczema in babies usually appears in the first year, and usually gets better as they grow older. There are two main types of eczema in babies. The eczema that causes cradle cap (below) and nappy rash (p46) is the most common type. It's not itchy and doesn't really affect the child much. However, infantile eczema is usually due to an allergic reaction and can be very irritating and sore. Eczema is not infectious.

Signs and symptoms of infantile eczema

Dry, sore, red, scaly skin.
Very itchy.
Small watery blisters.
Affects any part of the body but creases in the skin (e.g. underside of the elbows, behind the knees) are most often affected. Infantile eczema may be made worse by stress, illness (e.g. colds, fever), or even teething.

Prevention

Eczema can be linked to allergies to food or other substances (e.g. soap powders, pet hairs), and you should discuss these with your nurse or doctor. If there is a specific allergy that runs through your family, the cause may be the same for your child's eczema.

Home treatment

If the rash is mild and doesn't hurt your baby, you can easily treat it at home. Don't use harsh soaps, baby oil or baby bath lotion. Use emulsifying ointments from your pharmacist to clean and moisturise your baby's skin. Use light material for your baby's clothes and bed (e.g. cotton rather than wool or nylon). Contact the *National Eczema Society,* p60, for further information and advice.

Consult your doctor if:

■ The rash is widespread, spreading, or inflamed and 'weepy', or if your baby or child has a high fever (see p46).

Cradle cap

Cradle cap is a mild form of eczema that causes peeling skin on the scalp, which forms a thick, cap-shaped layer. The condition neither harms nor worries the baby.
Home treatment: Cradle cap can be simply treated. Gently rub the affected parts of the scalp with olive oil, leave it on overnight and then wash it off with a mild shampoo in the morning. Alternatively, gently rub baby oil or petroleum jelly into the scalp and then gently wash it off.

Nappy rash

A baby's sensitive skin often gets chapped by the rubbing of the nappy, and this is made worse by urine and faeces. Nappy rash is very common, and you can do a lot to reduce the severity or prevent it completely.

Home treatment and Prevention:
- Change the nappy whenever it's dirty. Don't use wipes containing alcohol or moisturisers, instead use plenty of warm water.
- Treat the rash as soon as it appears with ointment from your pharmacist -

don't use talcum powder.
- Whenever possible, leave the nappy - and especially plastic pants - off.
- Re-usable nappies should be washed as directed by the manufacturer, but don't use strong household detergents.
- Don't use soap, baby lotion or baby bath solution. An emulsifying lotion for cleaning and moisturising the skin is available from your pharmacist.

An angry red rash that doesn't clear up when you follow the steps above, and which goes beyond the nappy area may be a fungal infection (see 'Thrush', below).

Thrush

Thrush can occur in babies, either as thick white patches on the tongue or inside of the mouth, or as redness or thick white patches in the nappy area.

Home treatment: Thrush is not serious and can be easily treated at home with anti-fungal creams available from your pharmacist (remember that different creams are used for the mouth or nappy area).

Fits, FEVERS AND HIGH TEMPERATURES

Fits (see 'Signs and symptoms' below) in children who are 6 months to 4 years old are usually caused by high body temperature. They are common and it does not mean that your child will continue to have fits during their life. If your child has a fit for the first time, you should see your doctor. Also, if your child loses consciousness when there is no high temperature or fever, you should see your doctor, as it may be a sign of epilepsy.

Fever is usually a sign of illness; e.g. in viral infections like colds and flu. Fever by itself is not harmful. The temperature of babies can also rise above their normal temperature if they are too warm or even if they are teething.

Signs and symptoms of fits
- Slight to violent shaking.
- Baby may go blue in the face.
- Confusion before and afterwards, with drowsiness afterwards.

- Incontinence (bladder or bowel movements that can't be controlled).
- High temperature.

Causes
Any illness causing a temperature higher than 39°C (102F)can cause a convulsion. Other causes include infections, some medicines, poisons, and very rarely vaccinations or epilepsy.

Home treatment/Prevention

Reducing fever: If your baby or child has a temperature, try to lower it by removing all heavy clothing, and wiping the skin with a sponge soaked in lukewarm water. Continue trying to reduce fever in this way until the temperature reaches 38.5°C (101F) or less. Give a simple painkiller like sugar free paracetamol for children.

If your child has a fit, don't try to restrain them, let it happen naturally and mply remove any hard or sharp objects. ponge the child with lukewarm water to ring down the temperature. Roll the child nto his or her side in the recovery position (see p5). **Never put anything in the mouth of someone having a fit,** and don't give them anything to eat or drink until they are completely better.

Consult your doctor if:

- It's the first fit for a baby or child
- There is any sign of choking
- The fits continue even after sponging with luke warm water
- There is any sign of meningitis (below)
- There are repeated fits or loss of consciousness that is not linked to high temperature or fever.

Although you should phone your doctor if your child has a fit, less than half of all children who suffer a fit will ever have another one.

Fever and temperatures - when to phone your doctor for advice.

- Babies under 1 year - temperature of 38.5°C/101F or higher.
- Children over 3 years and adults - temperature of 39°C/102F for over 24 hours.

Remember temperature varies among individuals. Babies especially can be affected by too many warm clothes or a hot environment. A good check to see if babies really need to see a doctor is *Baby Check* (see p60).

➡ **Colds and flu - p22**
➡ **Fits and convulsions - p8**

➡ **Recovery position - p5**

MENINGITIS

Meningitis is not a common ailment but a thankfully rare illness that needs urgent attention. It is important, however, to be aware of the symptoms, which can easily be mistaken for flu or a bad cold, especially in some babies and young children. If you are not sure, call your doctor immediately for advice. Vaccinations against one type of meningitis (Hib) in childhood will protect your child against this form of the disease (see p14). For more information, contact the *National Meningitis Trust* (see p61).

If you suspect meningitis, the safest option is to go straight to your nearest hospital Accident and Emergency (A&E) department. Your GP will advise on the telephone but time is important.

Signs and symptoms

Babies and very young children should be taken to A&E if:

- They are difficult to wake
- Their cry is high pitched and different from normal
- They vomit repeatedly not just after feeds
- They refuse feeds, either from the bottle, breast or by spoon
- Their skin appears pale or blotchy, especially with red or blue-black bruises that don't go white when you press your finger or a glass tumbler on them
- The soft spot on top of your baby's head (called the fontanelle) is tight or bulging.

Remember, a fever may not be present.

Signs to look out for in older children:

- A constant headache
- A high temperature
- Vomiting
- Drowsiness or confusion
- Dislike of bright lights, daylight or even the TV
- Neck stiffness. Moving their chin to their chest will be very painful
- A rash of red/blue spots or bruises which don't go white when you press with a glass tumbler.

Measles, mumps and rubella

Measles, mumps and rubella (german measles) were once common childhood illnesses but are thankfully now quite rare due to immunisation (see p14). You should call your nurse or doctor immediately for advice if you suspect your child has one of these illnesses.

Measles: High fever (p46), runny nose and hacking cough, red eyes, and spotty rash over the body.
Mumps: Swelling and tenderness in the glands on one or both sides of the face, sore throat, fever (see p46) and vomiting.
Rubella: Fine pink rash that starts on face and then covers the entire body, slight fever, and swollen neck glands.

➡ **Fever - p46**
➡ **Vaccination schedule - p14**
➡ **Useful contacts - p61**

Teething

Discomfort can occur in young babies when new teeth come through. Offer the baby something hard to chew on (e.g. a teething ring), spread a sugar-free teething gel over the gums (available from your pharmacy) or give the baby a sugar-free infant paracetamol syrup.

VOMITING IN INFANTS AND CHILDREN

Vomiting is common in babies and young children and can happen even though there is nothing wrong with the food they've eaten. Babies normally vomit up small mouthfuls of milk immediately after feeding, and occasional vomiting is not a problem. However, if the child vomits often or very heavily it may indicate something wrong.

Causes and complications

Vomiting may be caused by a lot of coughing, eating or drinking too quickly, or a viral infection. In babies and young children, care must be taken to avoid too much water loss (dehydration) with repeated vomiting, as well as choking on the vomit.

Prevention

To help prevent vomiting, follow closely the directions for making up feeds and sterilise the equipment completely. Burp your baby well before laying down.

Home treatment

Babies
Stop giving milk and solids for 24 hours, instead give a glucose and mineral solution, available from your pharmacist. After 24 hours, slowly start breast feeding or bottle feeding again (for formula feeds, dilute them with half water until the vomiting stops).

Children over 1 year
■ Reassure the child and support them while they vomit. Wipe a cool flannel over their face afterwards.
■ If vomiting has continued for a while, give them an oral rehydration solution (ORS) – available from your pharmacist.
■ Once the fluids stay down, move on to rice or plain toast - don't give dairy products (see p32).

WIND AND COLIC

Wind is most common after feeding and is usually caused by air being taken in with the feed. In the case of bottle feeding, a teat hole that is too small can cause the baby to swallow air which will cause wind.

Colic is a term used to describe the discomfort that causes young babies to cry excessively. This is often linked with feeding. It is most common in 2 week old babies and occurs in babies up to about 3 months old. Usually, colic attacks start in the evening. They are harmless, but can be upsetting to parents.

Signs and symptoms of colic

- Distressed crying, with baby difficult to calm down - often worse in the evenings, when they wake up, or after a feed.
- Baby turning red and drawing up the legs.
- Convulsive movements.

Causes of colic

Often there will be no obvious reason for a colic attack. It may be due to one or more of the following:
- Tiredness, tension or not enough breast milk from the mother
- Food allergy
- Too much wind
- Not enough sleep or disturbance from a busy and noisy home.

Home treatment/Prevention

Wind
- Sit your baby up during feeds to prevent them swallowing air.
- Burp your baby at regular times during the feed.
- For bottle-fed babies, check the teat size - it should give about one drop per second. Try a larger size if your baby is an 'eager' feeder.

Colic
- Breast feeding is the best option for preventing colic, but mothers must be careful not to drink too much caffeine.
- Carry your baby close to you in a sling when you can.
- Get enough rest. Babies are sensitive to tension in parents and this may cause them to cry.
- In the event of a colic attack, check your baby is not hungry, wet or cold. Soothe your baby in the usual way (e.g. rock, sing, give a dummy etc.)

Self-help groups like Serene will also be able to give you information and advice (see p61).

WOMEN'S HEALTH

Most common female ailments can easily be dealt with at home, and women can do a lot to prevent more serious diseases (see 'Attending for health screening', p15). *Women's Health* and the other organisations listed on p61 will be able to give you further information, including details of other women's health groups and services.

CYSTITIS

Cystitis, or bladder infection, affects women more often than men. Women are more likely to get cystitis during pregnancy or after the menopause. You should see your doctor if you think you have a bladder infection (see 'Consult your doctor if'), but in the meantime you can take steps to relieve the symptoms.

Signs and symptoms
- Wanting to pass water, but little or no urine when you try to urinate.
- Pain or burning when you urinate.
- Dull ache in lower stomach.
- Fever.
- Urine bloodstained or cloudy and foul-smelling.

Causes and complications
Cystitis is usually due to an infection caused by bacteria from the anus, which are transferred to the urinary tract. Cystitis must be taken seriously as it can lead to kidney problems if it's not treated.

Prevention
- Drink plenty of water.
- Wipe from front to back after going to the toilet.
- Wash your hands before inserting tampons.
- Wash your genital area before and after having sex.
- Wash your genital area morning and night, and encourage your partner to do the same.

Home treatment

- Drink ½ litre (about three medium glasses) of water straight away, then ¼ litre (one and a half medium glasses) every 20 minutes until you are producing large amounts of urine. This helps flush out the bacteria from the bladder.
- Take a potassium or sodium citrate solution - available from your pharmacist. Alternatively, take a teaspoon of bicarbonate of soda in water every hour for the first 3 hours, and then three times a day (if you are taking other medicines or have high blood pressure or heart problems, first check with your doctor).
- To ease the pain, hold a hot water bottle against your stomach, or have a warm bath.
- Take simple painkillers like paracetamol or soluble aspirin, if needed.

Consult your doctor if:
- You may have a bladder infection
- An attack of cystitis lasts for longer than a day or two, or if you have repeated attacks
- You are pregnant
- You notice blood in your urine
- You also have vaginal soreness, irritation or discharge.
- You have increased thirst

Take a urine sample with you to the surgery. This should be from your first visit to the toilet in the morning (use a clean, well rinsed bottle).

 ➡ **Useful contacts - p61**

PAINFUL PERIODS

Most women have some discomfort or pain during their periods. The pain is usually worse at the beginning of a period, and slowly gets better over the next couple of days. Oral contraceptives reduce period pain in most women.

Signs and symptoms

- Dull ache or pain in the lower back and/or stomach.
- Cramp-like pains in the lower stomach that come in waves and may be very bad.
- Nausea and vomiting.
- Diarrhoea.
- Headache.

Causes and complications

Period pain is usually due to the womb muscle contracting. It does not pose a serious threat.

Home treatment/Prevention

- Take soluble aspirin or ibuprofen as soon as the pain starts, and then in regular doses (follow the directions on the label). If you can't use these drugs for any reason, try paracetamol.
- Take a warm bath, or hold a hot water bottle or warm towel over the painful area.
- Gently massage the painful area.
- Sip hot drinks.
- Take gentle exercise to help the blood flow.

Consult your doctor if:
- The pain is unbearable, or the pattern of pain is different from usual
- You also have a fever
- Your period is very heavy or there is any unusual vaginal discharge.

Menstrual problems

Other menstrual problems are much less common, and should be discussed with your doctor. These include:

Absent periods. The most common reason for women of reproductive age not to have periods is pregnancy. However, if a girl's periods do not start by the age of 15, or if periods suddenly stop, she should see a doctor.

Heavy periods. Each woman has her own 'normal' amount of bleeding, so you will notice if your pattern changes. This can include: heavier than usual periods, large blood clots in the flow, bleeding for longer than usual. If you have several heavy periods, go and see your doctor.

Irregular periods. Periods are often irregular in young girls and after childbirth. In other cases, see your doctor if you experience heavy bleeding between periods (many women have spotting between periods which is not serious), bleeding more often than usual or in an irregular pattern, bleeding after intercourse or after menopause.

Pregnancy

A woman who suspects she is pregnant should visit her doctor as soon as possible; also, see 'Planning a pregnancy ', p15. Pregnancy is not dealt with in depth here. There are however many books and magazines generally available.

➡ Useful contacts - p61

PRE-MENSTRUAL SYNDROME (PMS)

Nearly half of all menstruating women get pre-menstrual syndrome (PMS), also known as pre-menstrual tension (PMT). This causes a range of symptoms during the 7-10 days before a period starts.

Signs and symptoms

Symptoms of PMS vary. The most common are:
- Irritability, anxiety, depression without any real reason
- Loss of concentration
- Feeling hostile and angry
- Bloated feeling in lower abdomen
- Tenderness or tightness in the breasts
- Headache
- Swelling of ankles and hands
- Weight gain
- Craving for certain foods, especially sweet, rich things (e.g. chocolate).

A test to help you find if you have PMS is:

- Do the same symptoms occur each month?
- Do the symptoms improve or go away once you start bleeding?
- Do you have at least one week without any symptoms every month?

Causes

Hormone changes that occur during the menstrual cycle are thought to cause PMS. It can affect your quality of life, but there is a lot you can do to help reduce the symptoms.

Home treatment/Prevention

- Eat smaller meals every 3-4 hours with plenty of whole grains, fruit and vegetables. Reduce your salt, fat and sugar intake (see p11).
- Avoid drinks with caffeine (e.g. colas, coffee, tea) or alcohol.
- Increase your level of activity (see p13).
- Take simple painkillers like paracetamol, soluble aspirin or ibuprofen if you need them.
- The oral contraceptive pill helps some women.
- Taking evening primrose oil or starflower oil may help
- Talk to others around you, your PMS also affects those you live and work with.

The *National Association for Premenstrual Syndrome* (p61) will be able to provide you with more information.

Consult your doctor if:
- The symptoms are badly affecting your normal life
- You feel depressed all the time, or feel like hurting yourself or someone else.

 ➡ **Useful contacts - p61**

THRUSH

Thrush is a very common complaint, which can affect babies and adult men (especially men who are not circumcised) as well as women. Although it's unpleasant, thrush is not harmful and can be treated using medicines from your pharmacist.

Signs and symptoms

In women:
- Thick white vaginal discharge that looks like cottage cheese and smells yeasty.
- Redness, itchiness and soreness around the vagina and bottom.
- Hot feeling in vagina.
- Pain during sex.
- Pain or burning when you urinate.

Symptoms in men include:
- Itching, burning or irritation at the tip of the penis (or under the foreskin)
- Redness or red patches at the tip of the penis (or under the foreskin)
- A thick, cheesy discharge under the foreskin, and slight discharge from the penis
- Discomfort when urinating.

Causes

Thrush is caused by a fungal infection of the vagina and genital area. In babies, it can appear in the mouth (see p46).

Prevention

Change underwear daily, and especially after exercise. Use cotton rather than nylon pants. Don't use harsh soaps or too much vaginal deodorant or perfumed bubble bath on your genital area. After going to the toilet, wipe from front to back.

Home treatment

- Use anti-fungal preparations (creams and pessaries) on the vaginal area. There is also a medicine you can take by mouth. These are available from your pharmacist.
- Treat your sexual partner as well, and don't have sex until the thrush is healed.
- Thrush in babies requires different treatment (see p46).
- Have a shower rather than a bath.

Your local *NHS Sexual Health (GUM) Clinic* (p61) will be able to give you more advice and help.

> ### Consult your doctor if:
> - The thrush does not get better with home treatment
> - You get repeated attacks
> - The vaginal discharge changes in smell or appearance
> - You have stomach pain
> - You are pregnant.

 ➡ **Useful contacts - p61**

Varicose veins

Varicose veins are swollen leg veins that usually occur on the calf or inside of the leg. They are common - especially in women after pregnancy and childbirth - and are not serious. Men also get them.
Prevention and Home treatment: Don't stand still for a long time, especially if you're pregnant. Sit with your legs on a footstool as often as you can to help the blood flow back up your legs. If you do have to stand for a long time, move your legs often and flex your calves. You can also wear support stockings (your nurse will show you how to put these on).
Consult your doctor if: the surrounding area is cracked or sore, or if your varicose veins worry you a lot.

SCREENING OUT WOMEN'S HEALTH PROBLEMS

Prevention is always better than cure, and if there is illness the earlier it's treated, the better. It's important for you to take steps to keep healthy, and help your doctor to catch any problems as early as possible. However, whether you attend for screening tests is ultimately your choice.

Cancer screening

Women can develop breast cancer and cervical cancer. It's important to protect your health by having the cervical smear tests offered by your surgery or local health centre. For more information about the cervical smear test, ask your doctor for a copy of the leaflet *Your smear test*. Also, be 'breast aware' and look out for any changes like a lump, thickening in the breast or armpit, an unusual feeling or pain, or discharge from the nipple. If you find a change that is unusual for you, contact your doctor as soon as possible. Breast screening is also offered to all women over 50 years old - it's advisable to go for these checks.

HEALTH AND THE MENOPAUSE

The menopause is the time when a woman's periods stop because she no longer makes enough hormones to stay fertile. It usually happens in women who are 45 to 55 years old, although it can happen earlier or later. The menopause can cause a number of symptoms. These include hot flushes, heavy sweating (especially at night) and dryness of the vagina. Many women are also more emotional than usual and may feel irritable and low, and get headaches. After the menopause, women have an increased chance of developing certain disorders like 'brittle bones' (osteoporosis) or heart problems. If the menopause worries you and your symptoms are causing you discomfort, talk to your doctor or practice nurse; your surgery may also have a *Well Women Clinic* for you to attend. There's also a lot you can do to help yourself:

- If you sweat at night, try lying on a large towel and use cotton night clothes and sheets. Keep a fan and bottle of cold water close at hand. Try deep breathing when a flush occurs
- Eating well is important for preventing osteoporosis (see p12)
- If you smoke, try to stop (see p10)
- Regular physical activity will help you feel better (see p13) and reduce the risk of osteoporosis
- If sex is painful because you have a dry vagina, try using a lubricant - available from your pharmacist
- Hormone replacement therapy (HRT) can help relieve menopausal symptoms - discuss this alternative with your doctor.

Osteoporosis

Osteoporosis develops gradually over many years, and usually there are no visible symptoms. It can occur in both men and women at any time, but it's most common in women from about 40 years. Brittle bones can cause pain, breaks and deformities such as a humped back.

Your best protection against osteoporosis is to build up your bones when you're young. You can do this by not smoking (p10), eating a healthy diet with plenty of calcium-rich foods (e.g. dairy products, sardines, peas/beans, green leafy vegetables), moderating your alcohol consumption (see p12), and doing weight-bearing activity (e.g. walking, dancing, tennis). Aim to keep up this lifestyle all your life. See your doctor if you think you may have osteoporosis, especially if someone else in your family has the condition. Your doctor can prescribe hormone replacement therapy (HRT) or some other medicines to help reduce further thinning of the bones. For more information contact the *National Osteoporosis Society*, p61.

Men's health

t's important for men to be aware of certain health risks that affect mainly
r only them.

IMPOTENCE

's normal for healthy men to have
ccasional problems getting or keeping an
rection, and it's nothing to worry about.
ut a continuous lack of satisfactory
rections (called impotence) can be very
psetting.

Causes and prevention

npotence can be caused by certain
rescription medicines (e.g. beta blockers
d antidepressants), heavy drinking, some
edical problems (e.g. diabetes, circulatory
seases and spinal injuries) and loss of
xual desire for your partner. Smoking also
akes impotence more likely. Avoiding the
uses can cut down the risk of impotence, but
certain to consult your doctor before stopping
y prescription medicines.

> ### Consult your doctor if:
> - You have a continuing problem that
>   won't go away.
>
> Don't be reluctant to discuss your
> problem with your doctors. A wide range
> of effective treatments is now available.
> Sexual counselling can also help.
> The *Impotence Association* (p61) will be
> able to give you further advice on treatment.

➡ Useful contacts - p61

Hair loss

Most men, including young men,
naturally lose some hair as they grow
older. Hair loss can also be due to
ringworm which can be treated with
antifungal lotion from your pharmacists
(see p38). Patchy baldness (known as
alopecia areata) can occur on any part of
the body and can also affect women and
children. The cause is unknown but the
hair usually grows back without
treatment in about 6-9 months.

The options for permanent hair loss
include transplants or wearing a wig,
which can be expensive, or a lotion that
you apply to the balding surface
(available from your pharmacist).

PROSTATE PROBLEMS

ostate problems are common in men over
e age of 50. The prostate gland gets bigger
th age. This growth is not due to cancer, but
an affect the flow of urine, causing a
mber of symptoms, known as benign
ostatic hypertrophy (BPH). BPH is very
mmon. Prostate cancer can also occur and
can give similar symptoms to BPH. (Your
doctor will give you a physical examination
and also a blood test to rule out prostate
cancer.) Visit your doctor as soon as possible if
you have any of the symptoms of BPH listed
overleaf. BPH and prostate cancer are both
more easily treated if they are caught early.

Signs and symptoms of BPH

- Poor flow of urine.
- Frequent trips to the toilet, especially at night.
- A feeling of 'not quite emptying the bladder'.
- Trouble starting the urine flow, and dribbling at the end of urination.

Causes and complications of BPH

The cause of BPH is not fully understood, although a diet low in protein, and high in carbohydrate and fat may contribute. If it's not treated, BPH can prevent you emptying the bladder properly and this can cause kidney problems.

Prevention

There are no specific steps that can prevent BPH or prostate cancer, but keeping to a healthy body weight (see p11) and eating a good diet can cut down your risk. Cut down the fat you eat (especially animal fats), and eat lots of fresh fruits (especially citrus fruits) and vegetables like carrots every day (see p12).

Consult your doctor if:

- You notice any problems passing urine
- There is any blood in your urine or sperm.

TESTICLE PROBLEMS

Problems with the testicles are fortunately quite rare, but they can be serious. Testicular cancer is the biggest cause of cancer-related death in men who are 18 to 35 years. But if it's discovered early it is completely curable, so it's important to know how to detect the signs.

Signs and symptoms

- A lump on one testicle.
- Pain. tenderness or hardness in either testicle.
- Unusual discharge from the penis.
- Blood in the sperm at ejaculation.

Causes and complications

There is no single cause of testicular cancer, but your chance of getting it is increased if you have an undescended (absent) testicle, or if it runs in your family.

Prevention

Men should check their testicles once a month after a warm bath or shower.This makes the skin of the scrotum softer so it's easier to feel the testes.

Consult your doctor if:

- You feel anything out of the ordinary. Remember, cancer is often painless, so don't delay.
- You develop pain in the testicle(s)

Checking your testicles

Cradle the scrotum in the palm of your hand and using both hands, gently roll each testicle in turn between your thumb and forefinger. Feel carefully for any lumps or swellings. The testicles should both be smooth except along the top and back, where you will feel the tube which carries sperm to the penis. Also, one testicle will probably feel bigger and lower than the other one. This is completely normal. Contact *Testicular Self Examination* or your local *NHS Sexual Health (GUM) Clinic* (p61) for more information.

THE HOME MEDICINE CHEST

We never know when minor
illnesses are going to strike or
accidents occur, so it's worth
being prepared. A few simple
remedies kept together in a
secure place, out of the reach of
children will enable you to cope
with most minor ailments and
incidents.

The Home Medicine Chest
- Paracetamol/soluble aspirin/ibuprofen
- Paracetamol and/or ibuprofen syrups
  for children
- Decongestant for adding to hot water,
  e.g. menthol
- Decongestant for children
- Mild laxative
- Oral rehydration solution; anti-diarrhoeal
- Indigestion remedy, e.g. antacids
- Antiseptic solution
- Sunscreen - SPF15 or higher
- Sunburn treatment, e.g. calamine
- Travel sickness tablets
- Thermometer

Basic first aid items
- A selection of 20 plasters in assorted
  sizes
- six medium, two large and two extra-
  large sterile dressings
- triangular bandages
- two sterile eye pads
- cotton wool, safety pins, tweezers,
  sharp scissors and disposable gloves

What to keep in the Home Medicine Chest

Your medicine chest should include a pain killer such as paracetamol, soluble aspirin or ibuprofen. If children are likely to be treated, remember to keep paracetamol or ibuprofen syrup (preferably sugar free) made specifically for them, and **never give aspirin to children under 12 years.**

You may also want to keep a **decongestant** to relieve catarrh, sinusitis and dry cough by adding it to hot water as directed on the bottle, and inhaling the steam. Remember that children may need a different type or dose of decongestant from adults, or they may be treated simply by sitting them in a steam-filled bathroom.

Stomach upsets can affect anyone from time to time. Sometimes you may need a **mild laxative** and at other times an **anti-diarrhoeal** agent. Keep both handy, as well as sachets of an **oral rehydration solution** to prevent the dehydration that can arise from diarrhoea or vomiting. **Antacids** are useful for treating occasional indigestion.

Antiseptic solution is useful for cleaning minor cuts and grazes – read the label as some antiseptics must be diluted in water before use.

Sun protection is vital for everyone, particularly children, keep a **sunscreen** of at least SPF15 available. If burning occurs, soothe the skin with a lotion like calamine. Calamine lotion is also useful for taking the sting and itch out of insect bites and stings.

You may want to keep some **travel sickness tablets** to hand, particularly if you are prone to travel sickness (not all tablets are suitable for everyone, read the label carefully).

Your medicine chest should also include a **thermometer**. And always have to hand the **basic first aid items** listed (see *First aid,* p5).

Other items for your medicine chest

Add any other items to your medicine chest that you are likely to need. For example, if you're prone to hayfever or allergies you may want to include antihistamine tablets (remember some of these cause drowsiness). If you take prescription medicines regularly, make sure you have enough and allow time for a new prescription if necessary.

Keep your copy of the *Home Healthcare Guide* with your medicines, so it's easily available when you need it. Use the space at the back of the book to note key contact details you're likely to need in an emergency.

Warning

- Keep the medicine chest in a secure, place, out of sight and reach of small children.
- Keep medicines in their original container.

- Always read the instructions and use the right dose.
- Don't keep or use medicines past their sell-by date (your pharmacist will throw these away for you)
- Don't share prescription medicines with others.

Holiday health

Nobody wants to think about getting sick on holiday, but by packing a few essential items, you can minimise the inconvenience if minor problems do arise.

The Holiday Kit

- Travel sickness tablets
- Paracetamol, including paracetamol and/or ibuprofen syrups for children
- Sunscreen - SPF15 or higher
- Sunburn treatment, e.g. calamine
- Plasters and antiseptic wipes
- Oral rehydration solution; anti-diarrhoeal
- Indigestion remedy, e.g. antacid

Other essentials, depending on your destination and needs

- Anti-malarial tablets (ask your pharmacist about the areas where you might need these)
- Insect repellent
- Water purification tablets
- Condoms/other contraceptives

Choose the medicines you take on holiday according to your needs. Always ensure you have enough of any prescription medicines. It's very important to check whether you need any vaccinations or malarial tablets before you travel. Your local doctor's surgery may have or be able to recommend a travel clinic, or you can contact a private clinic through an organisation such as *MASTA* (see p60). You may need several injections, so seek advice well in advance of departure.

Make sure you arrange medical insurance for your trip, and if you're travelling in the European Union, obtain a form E111 from the Post Office. Take this on holiday with you; it will entitle you to free or reduced cost medical care within EU member countries (be aware that the care can still be very expensive even with an E111 form).

➡ **First aid - p5**
➡ **Useful contacts - p60**

USEFUL CONTACTS

There are many hundreds of organisations and support services providing information and advice on health-related issues. The list here is by no means meant to be complete, rather it identifies some of the major groups that will be a useful first point of contact. If you can't find the organisation you need, call one of the organisations listed under *General information* who will be able to direct you to the organisation you need. Your local *Health Authority* (*Health Board* in Scotland and *Health and Social Services Board* in N. Ireland) or *Citizens Advice Bureau* (phone numbers in local phone book) will also be able to provide you with the details of local and national groups you can contact. Alternatively, use the Health Information Service below. Your pharmacy will be able to provide you with advice from a useful booklet *The pharmacy guide to self-help groups*.

Remember that many of the organisations have useful reading materials that they will provide you with free or at a small cost. Also, if you have access to the Internet, why not visit the websites listed, these often have lots of useful information.

General information

Community health council;
Local health council
(Scotland);
Central Services Agency
(N. Ireland)
number in local phone book

Department of Health
(Public Enquiry Office).
TEL: 0171 210 4850.
WEB: http://www.open.gov.
uk/doh/dhhome.htm

Health Information Service.
TEL: 0800 665544
WEB: http://www.
homepages.which.net/~colle
geofhealth\ index.htm

Health Education Authority
Customer Services.
TEL: 01235 465565
WEB: http://www.hea.
org.uk

Health Literature Line
(Department of Health).
TEL: 0800 555777
WEB: http://www.open.
gov.uk/doh/dhhome.htm

The Patient's Association.
TEL: 0181 423 8999
WEB: http://www.pat-assoc.
org.uk

Disabled people and carers

Carers' National Association.
TEL: 0345 573369
DIAL UK (disability advice).
TEL: 01302 310123
WEB: http://members.aol.com/
dialuk

Disabled Living Foundation
(advice primarily on disability
equipment).
TEL: 0870 603 9177
WEB: http://www.dlf.org.uk

Down's Syndrome Association.
TEL: 0181 682 4001

Royal National Institute For
Deaf People (RNID).
TEL: 0870 605 0123
MINICOM: 0171 296 8001

Royal National Institute for the
Blind (RNIB).
TEL: 0345 669999
WEB: http://www.rnib.org.uk

Royal Society for Mentally
Handicapped Children and
Adults (Mencap).
TEL: 0171 454 0454

Scope (Cerebral Palsy
Helpline).
TEL: 0800 626216
WEB: http://www.scope.org.uk

Drug abuse and addiction

Alcoholics Anonymous (AA).
TEL: 01904 644026

Drinkline (The National
Alcohol Helpline).
TEL: 0345 320202

Eating Disorders Association.
TEL: 01603 621414
WEB: http://www.gurney.org.
uk/eda/

National Drugs Helpline.
TEL: 0800 776600

QUIT (Smokers' Quitline).
TEL: 0800 002200

Older people

Age Concern.
TEL: 0181 679 8000
WEB: http://www.ace.org.uk

Counsel and Care
(information and advice for
people over 60).
TEL: 0845 300 7585

Help the Aged.
TEL: 0171 729 2229
WEB: http://www.helptheaged.
org.uk

Pennell Initiative for the Health
of Women in Later Life.
TEL: 0161 275 2901

First aid and accident prevention

British Red Cross.
TEL: 0171 235 5454
WEB: http://www.redcross.
org.uk

Child Accident Prevention
Trust. TEL: 0171 608 3828
WEB: http://www.qub.ac.
uk/cm/eph/capt/index.htm

The Chartered Society of
Physiotherapists.
TEL: 0171 306 6666

Royal Society for the
Prevention of Accidents.
TEL: 0121 248 2000

St John's Ambulance.
TEL: 0171 235 5231
WEB: http://www.st-john-
ambulance.org.uk

Health advice

Acne Support Group.
TEL: 0181 561 6868
WEB: http://www/m2w3.com/
acne/

Arthritis Care.
TEL: 0800 289170
WEB: http://www.vois.org.
uk/arthritiscare

British Allergy Foundation.
TEL: 0181 303 8525

British Dental Association.
TEL: 0645 551188
WEB: http://www.bda:
dentistry.org.uk

British Dental Health
Foundation.
TEL: 01788 546365
WEB: http://www.dentalhealth.
org.uk

British Diabetic Association.
TEL: 0171 636 6112
WEB: http://www.diabetes.
org.uk

British Digestive Foundation.
TEL: 0171 487 5332

British Dyslexia Association.
TEL: 01189 668271

British Epilepsy Association.
TEL: 0800 309030
WEB: http://www.epilepsy.
org.uk

British Heart Foundation.
TEL: 0171 935 0185
WEB: http://www.bhf.org.uk

British Nutrition Foundation.
TEL: 0171 404 6504

Cancerlink.
TEL: 0800 132905

Colon Cancer Concern.
TEL: 0171 381 4711

Community Hygiene Concern.
TEL: 0181 341 7167

Continence Foundation.
TEL: 0171 831 9831

Coronary Prevention Group.
TEL: 0171 580 1070
WEB: http://www.healthnet.
org.uk

Eye Care Information Service.
TEL: 0171 357 7730
WEB: http://www.eyeinfo.
co.uk/eyeinfo.

National Asthma Campaign.
TEL: 0345 010203
WEB: http://www.asthma.
org.uk

National Back Pain Association.
ADDRESS: 16 Elmtree Road,
Teddington, Middlesex,
TW11 8ST.
WEB: http://www.backpain.org

National Eczema Society.
TEL: 0990 118877
WEB: http://www.eczema.org

National Society for Research
into Allergies.
TEL: 01455 851546

Medical Advisory Service to
Travellers Abroad (MASTA).
TEL: 0891 224 100 (premium-
rate, 50p/minute). (For travel
information, also call the
Department of Health Public
Enquiry Line, p59).

Migraine Action Association
(previously British Migraine
Association).
TEL: 01932 352468
WEB: http://www.migraine.
org.uk

Psoriasis Association.
TEL: 01604 711129

Royal College of Speech and
Language Therapists.
TEL: 0171 613 6412

Royal Pharmaceutical Society
Information Centre.
TEL: 0171 735 9141

Stroke Association.
TEL: 0171 566 0330

Infants and children

Baby Check.
TEL: 01603 784400.

Child Growth Foundation.
TEL: 0181 995 0257

stic Fibrosis Trust.
EL: 0800 454482

auresis (Bedwetting) Resource
d Information Centre (ERIC).
EL: 0117 960 3060

oundation for the Study of
fant Deaths.
EL: 0171 235 1721
EB: http://www.vois.
g.uk/fsid

ational Meningitis Trust.
EL: 0345 538118

ational Society for the
evention of Cruelty to
ildren (NSPCC).
EL: 0800 800 500
EB. http://www.nspcc.org.uk

erene
xcessive crying and
eeplessness in infants).
EL: 0171 404 5011

Men's health
npotence Association.
EL.0181 767 7791
/EB: http://www.patient
upport.org.uk/infoindx.htm

rostate Help Association.
DDRESS: Langworth, Lincoln,
N3 5DF (include two 1st class
amps).
/EB: http://www.pha.u-
et.com

esticular Self Examination.
el: 01525 851313

Blood and organ donation
National Blood Donor
Service.
TEL: 0345 711711

British Organ Donor Society.
TEL: 01223 893636

Mental health
Cruse Bereavement Care.
TEL: 0181 332 7227

Depression Alliance.
TEL: 0171 633 0557
WEB: http://www.gn.apc.
org/da

SANE ('schizophrenia a
national emergency').
TEL: 0345 678000
WEB: http://www.mknco.uk/
help/charity/sane/index

The Samaritans.
TEL: 0345 909090

Sexual health & contraception
Brook Advisory Centres (advice
for young people on
contraception and pregnancy).
TEL: 0171 713 9000

Contraceptive Education
Service (CES) (advice on all
sexual health matters).
TEL: 0171 837 4044

Family Planning Association.
TEL: 0171 837 4044

Issue (National Fertility
Association).
TEL: 01922 722888
WEB: http://www.issue.co.uk

London Lesbian and Gay
Switchboard
TEL: 0171 837 7324
WEB: http://www.llgs.org.uk

National AIDS Helpline.
TEL: 0800 567123
WEB: http://www.nat.org.uk/nat/

NHS Sexual Health Clinics.
Look in your phonebook under
genito-urinary medicine
(GUM), sexually transmitted
diseases (STD) or venereal
diseases (VD).

Terrence Higgins Trust
Helpline (information on all
aspects of HIV and AIDS).
TEL: 0171 242 1010.
WEB: http://www.tht.org.uk

Women's health, pregnancy & childbirth
British Pregnancy Advisory
Service (abortion services and
advice on contraception and
abortion). TEL: 08457 304030
WEB: http://www.bpas.
demon.co.uk

Maternity Alliance.
TEL: 0171 588 8582

Miscarriage Association.
TEL: 01924 200799
WEB: http://www.btinternet.
com/~miscarriage.association/
ma/def

National Association for
Premenstrual Syndrome
(NAPS; includes advice on
postnatal depression).
TEL: 01732 741709

National Childbirth Trust (NCT).
TEL: 0181 922 8637

National Osteoporosis Society.
TEL: 01761 472721
WEB: http://www.nos.org.uk/
r.rowe/

Pennell Initiative for the Health
of Women in Later Life.
TEL: 0161 275 2901

Stillbirth and Neonatal Death
Society (SANDS).
TEL: 0171 436 5881
WEB: http://members.alo.com/
babyloss/sands.htm

Women's Aid.
(help for women experiencing
domestic violence)
TEL: 0345 023468

Women's Health.
TEL: 0171 251 6580

Women's Nationwide Cancer
Control Campaign.
TEL: 0171 729 2229
WEB: http://dspace.dial.pipex.
com/town/square/gm40

INDEX